"That love is inexhaustible, you will be there" **forever**

_____

_____

_____

_____

_____

THIS BOOK
Belongs to

_____

_____

Visit Our Author Page At

amazon.com

Scan me

Black Rose
PRESS HOUSE

LIGHTHOUSE COLORING BOOK

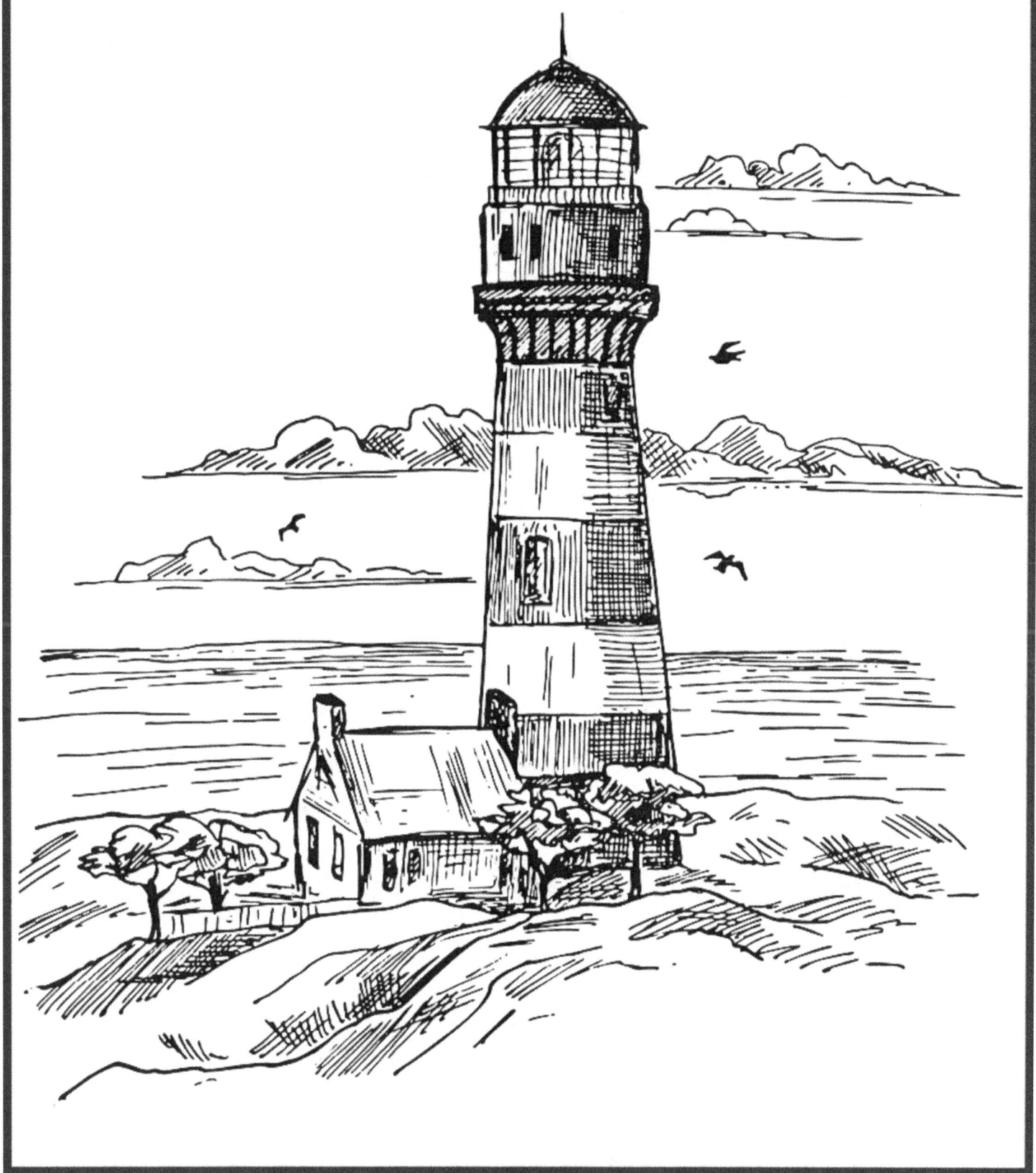

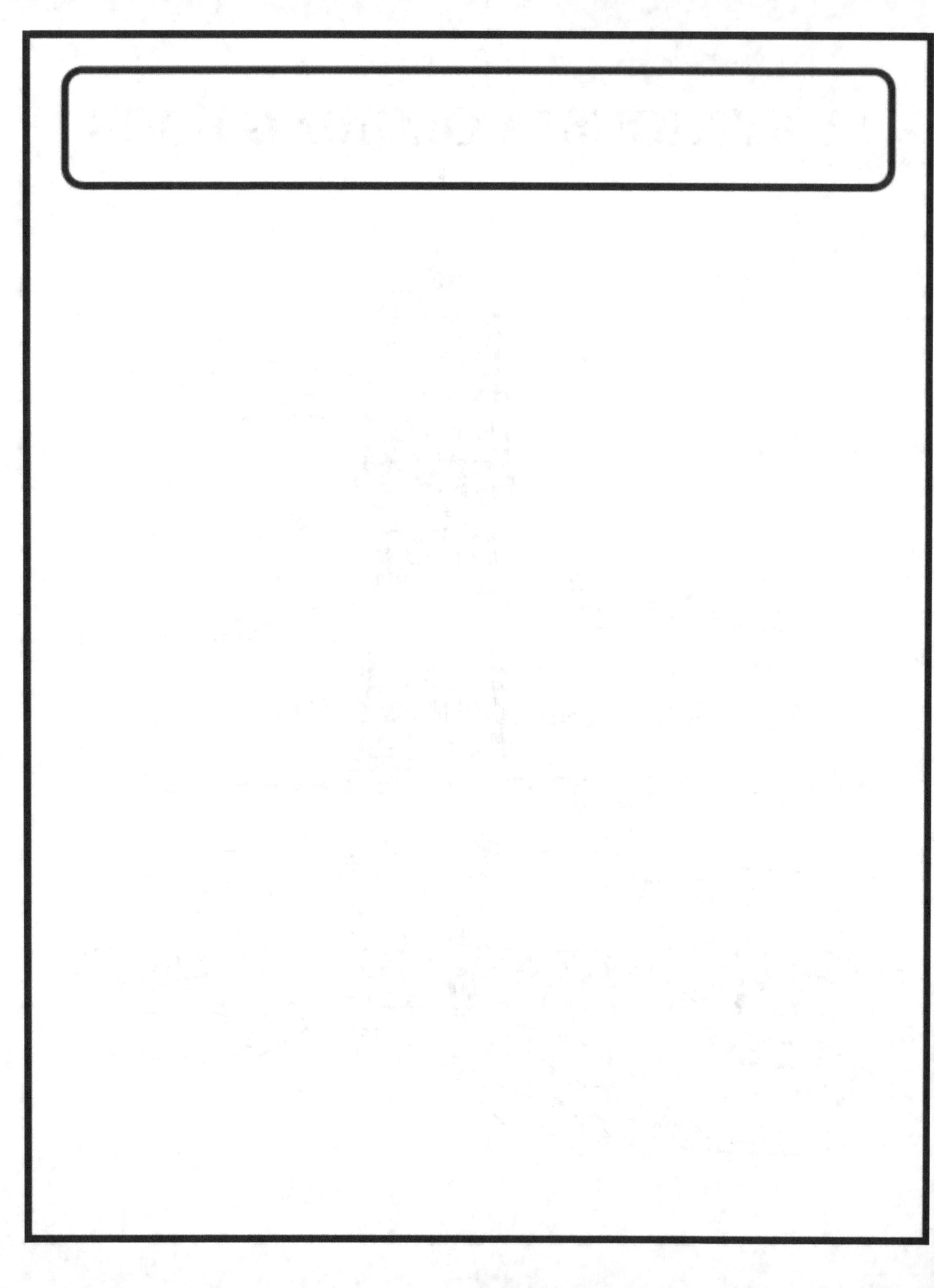

LIGHTHOUSE COLORING BOOK

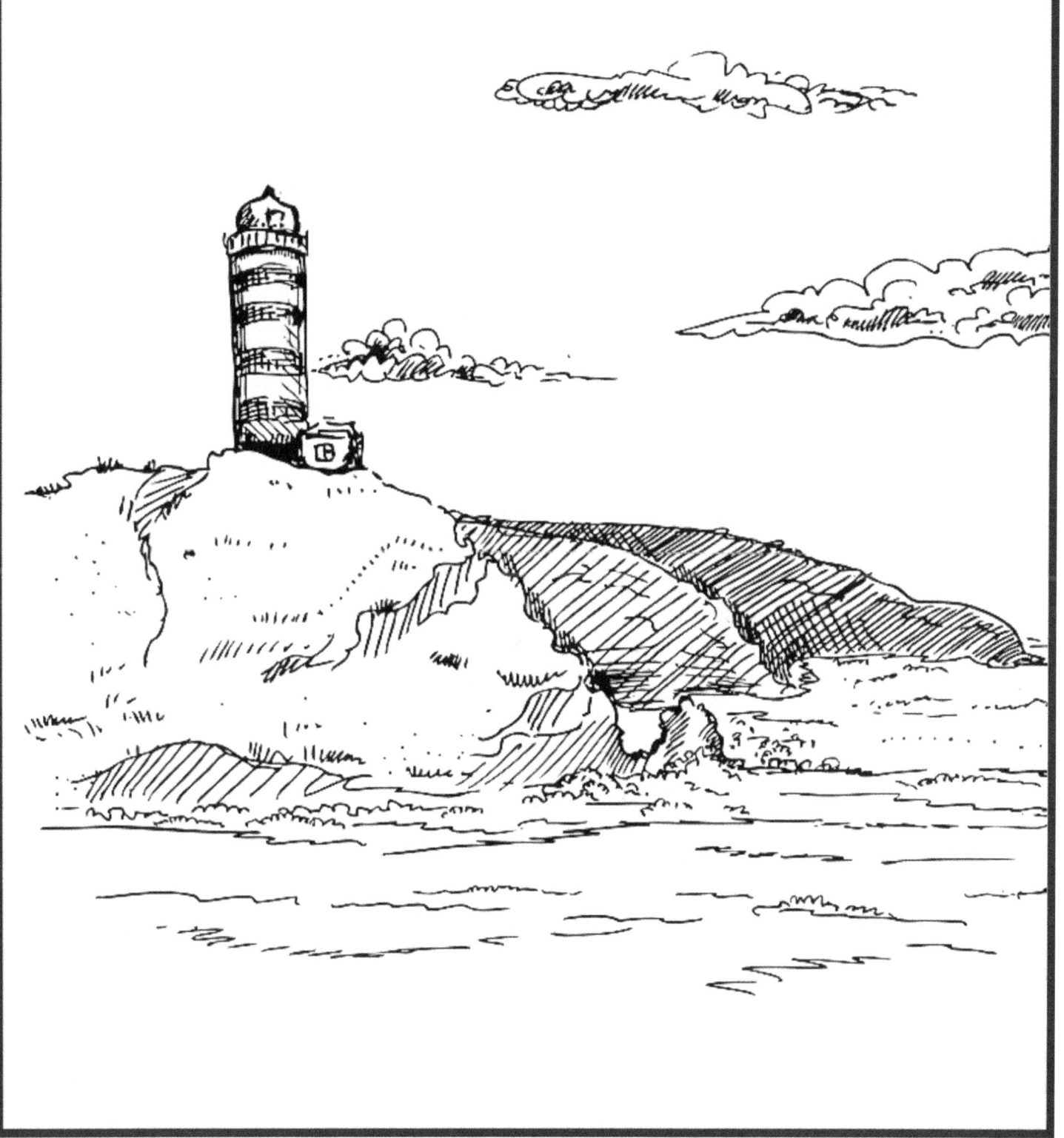

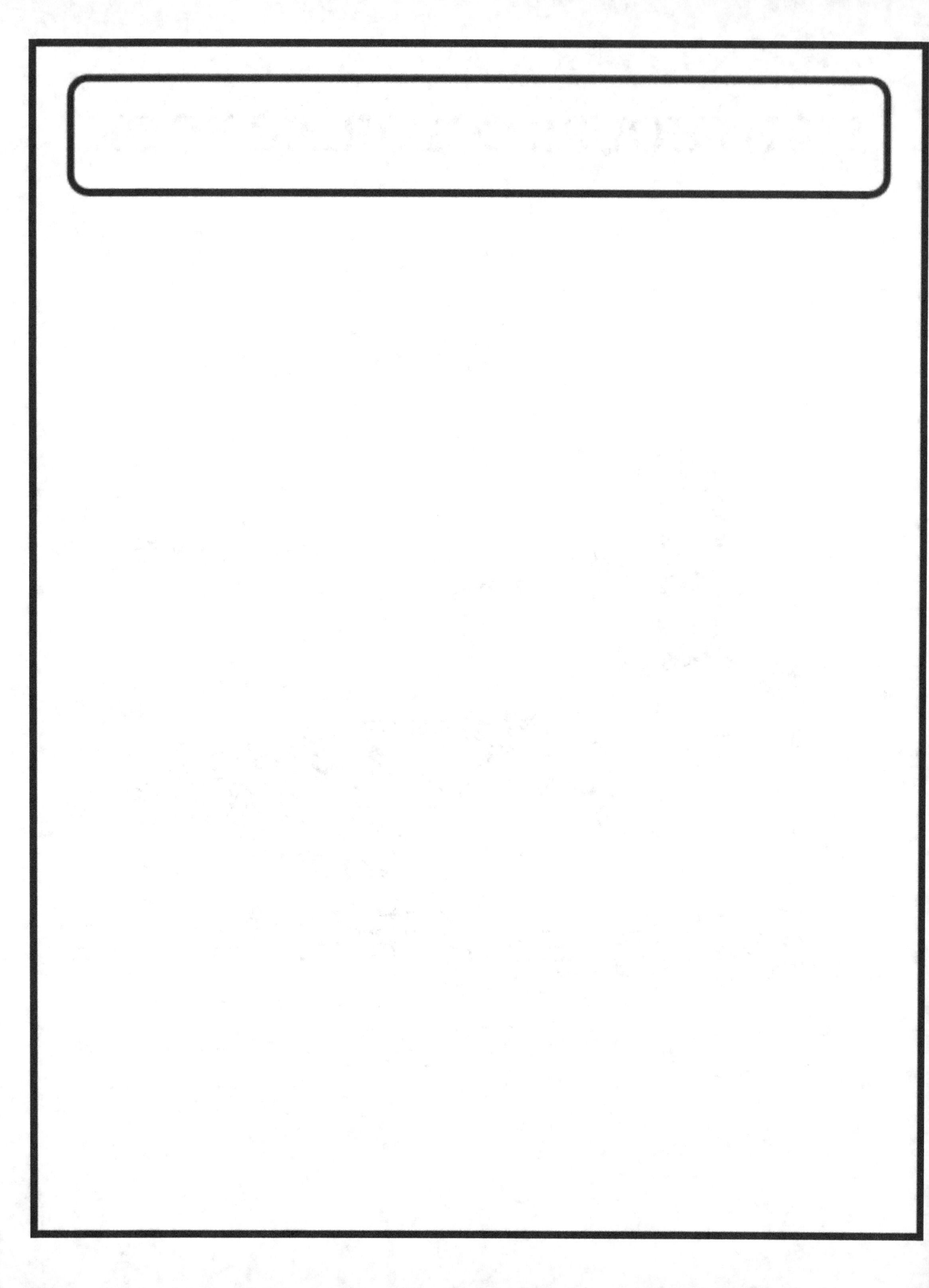

LIGHTHOUSE COLORING BOOK

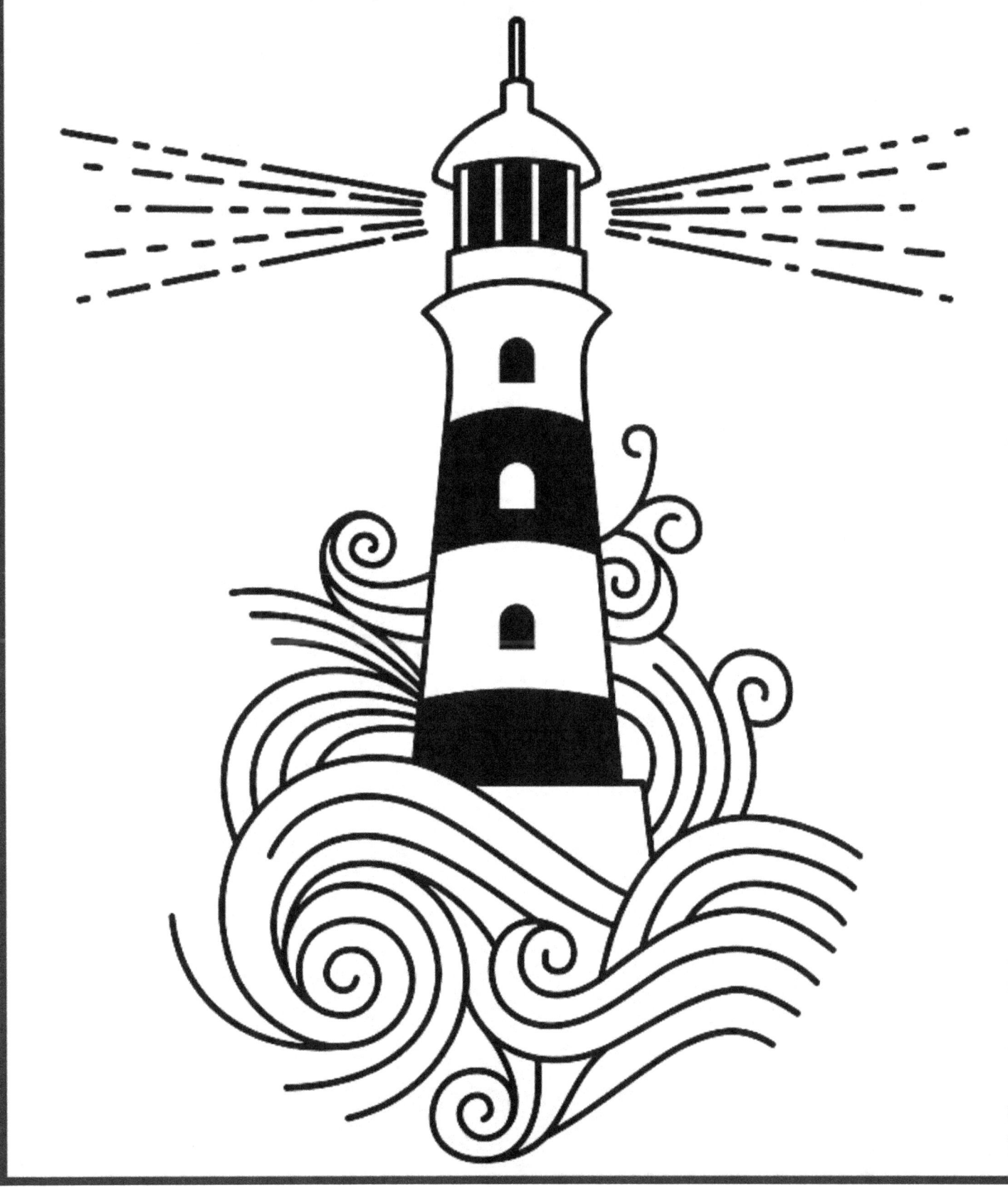

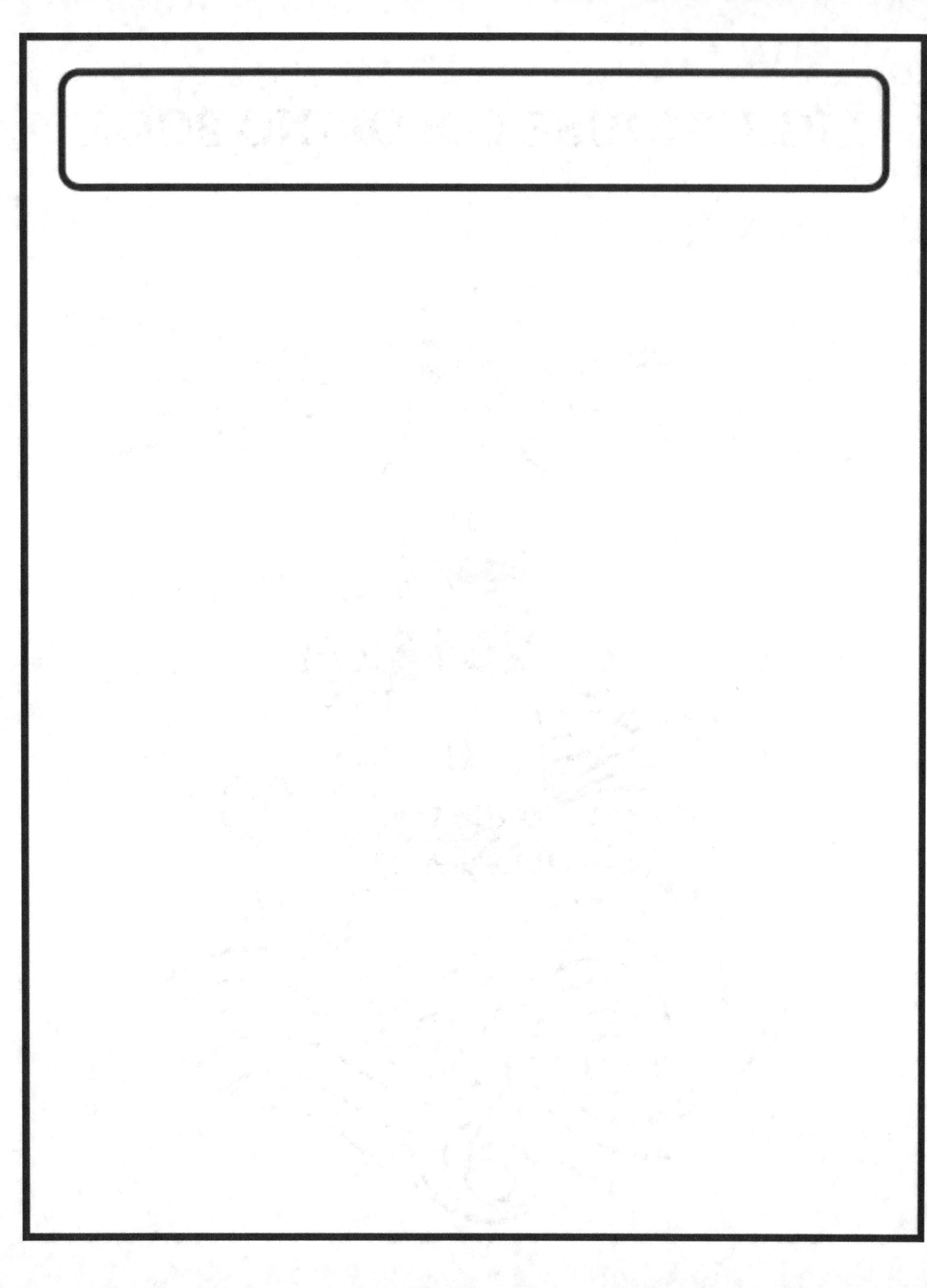

LIGHTHOUSE COLORING BOOK

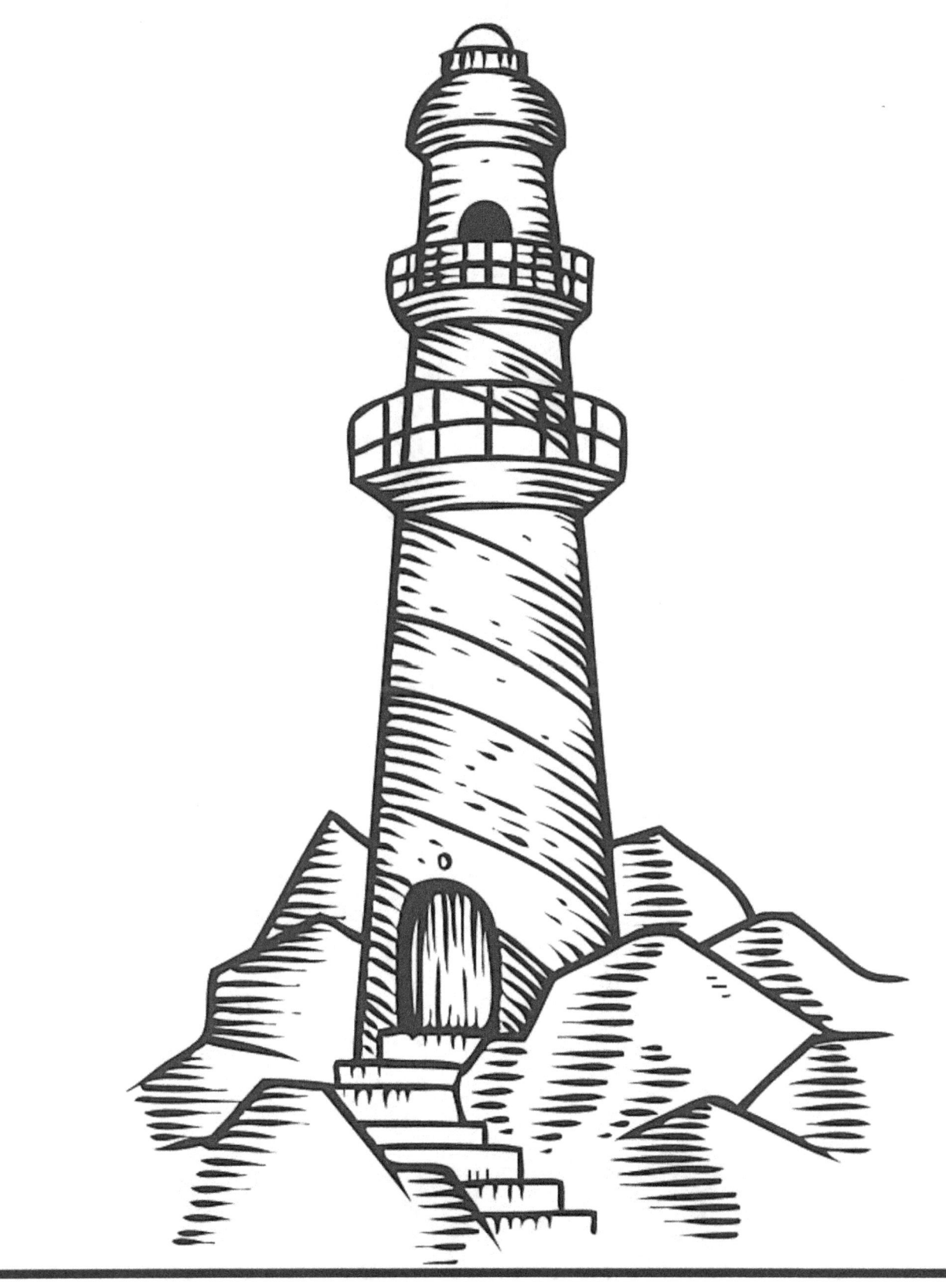

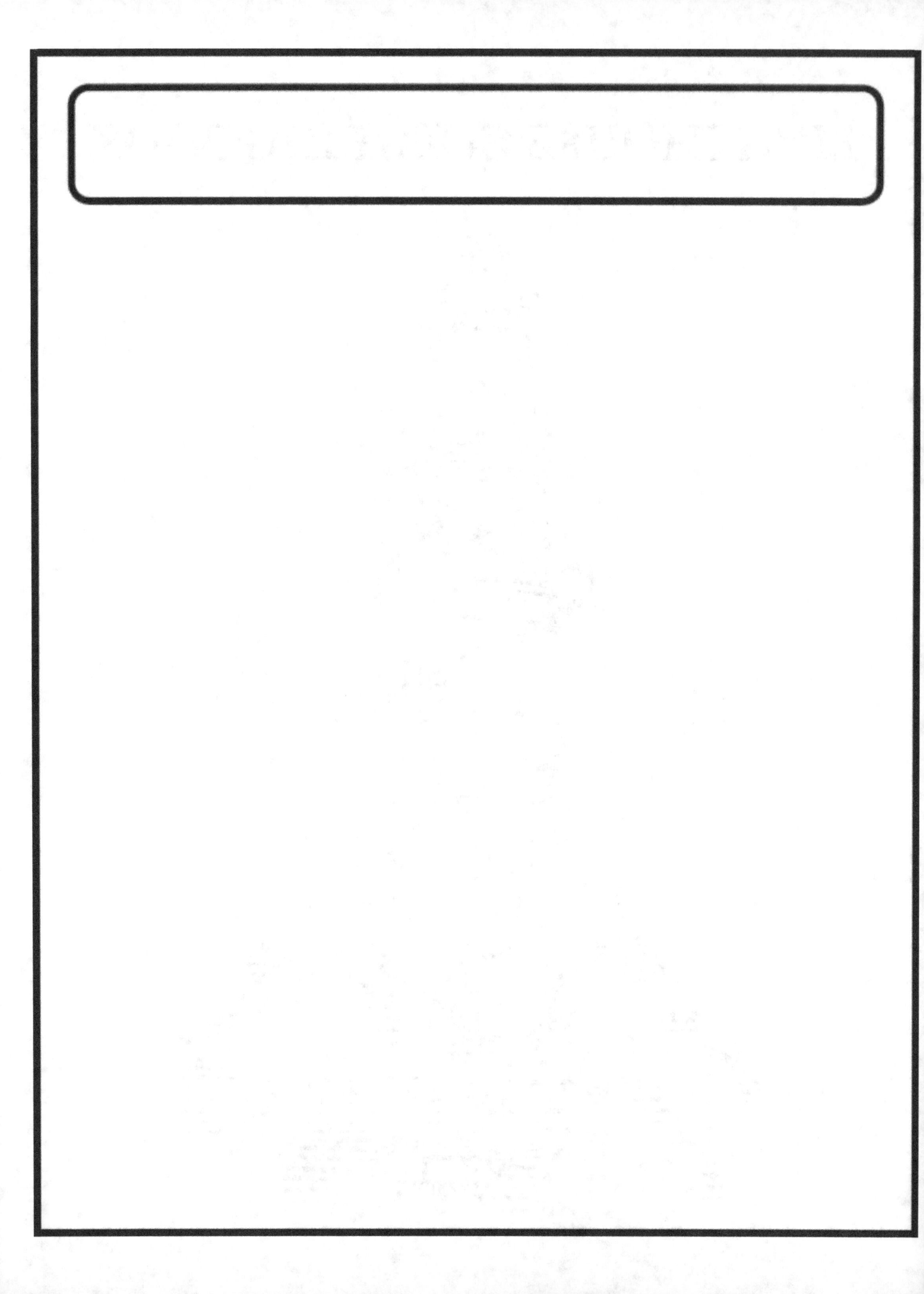

LIGHTHOUSE COLORING BOOK

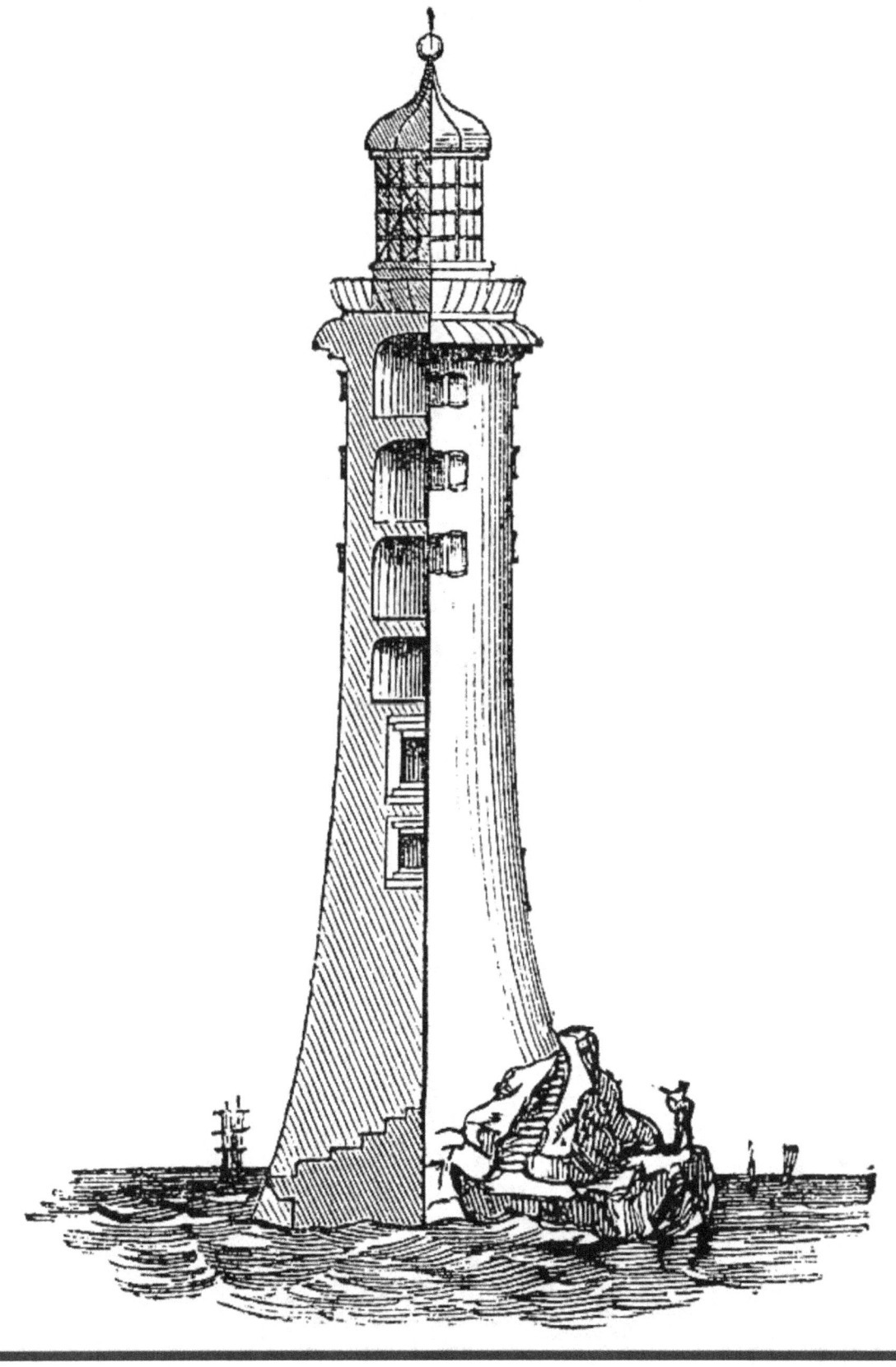

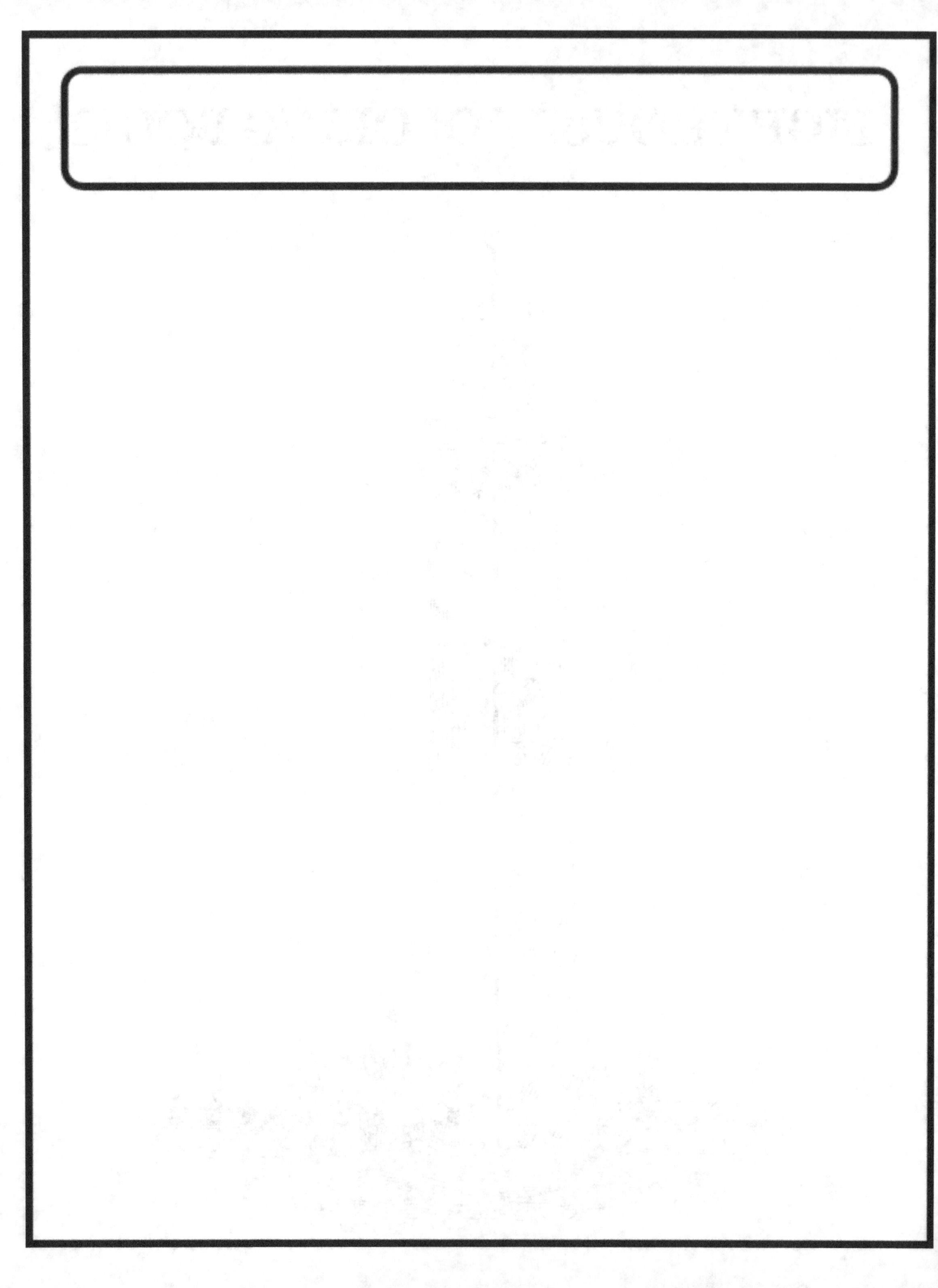

LIGHTHOUSE COLORING BOOK

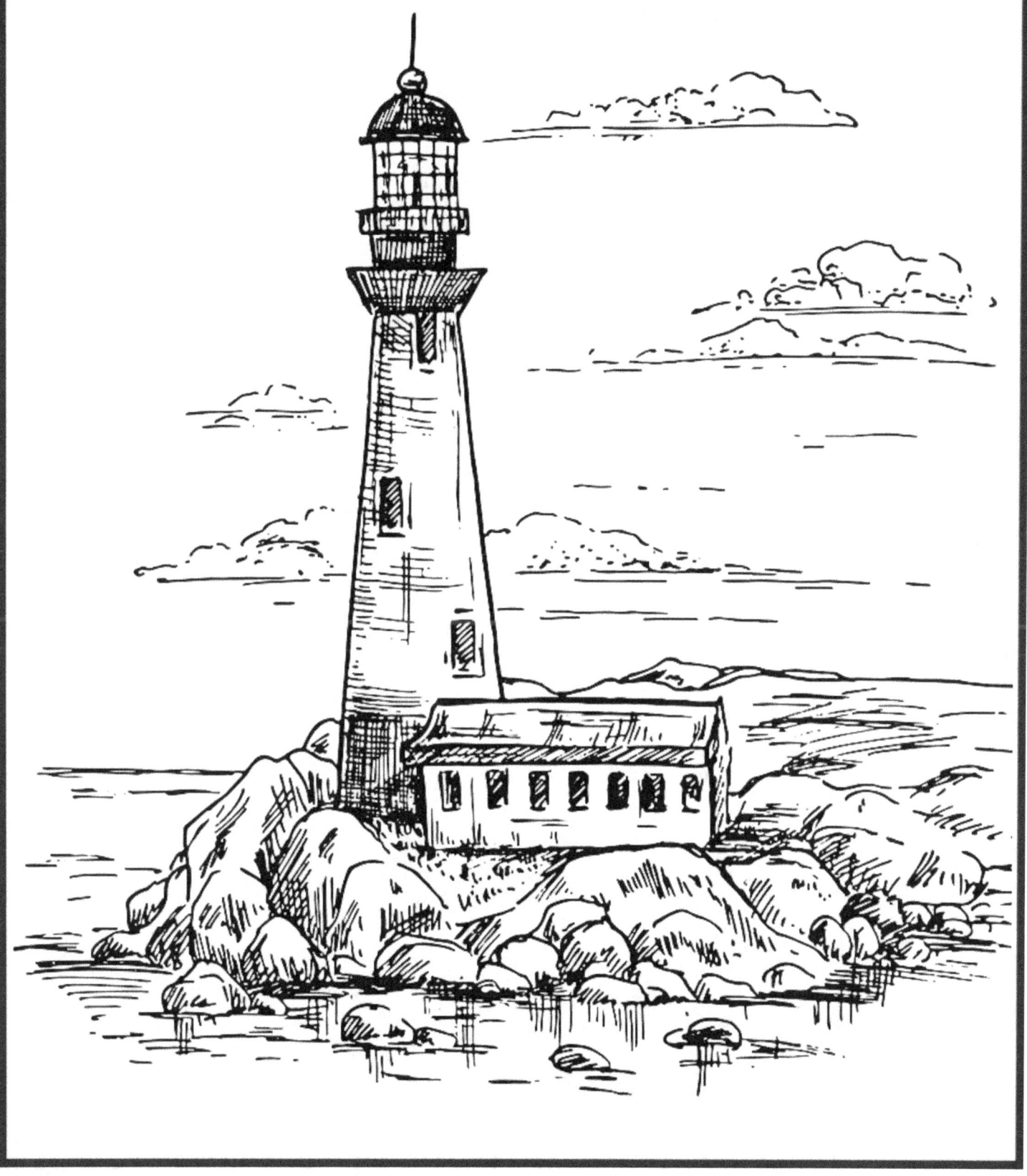

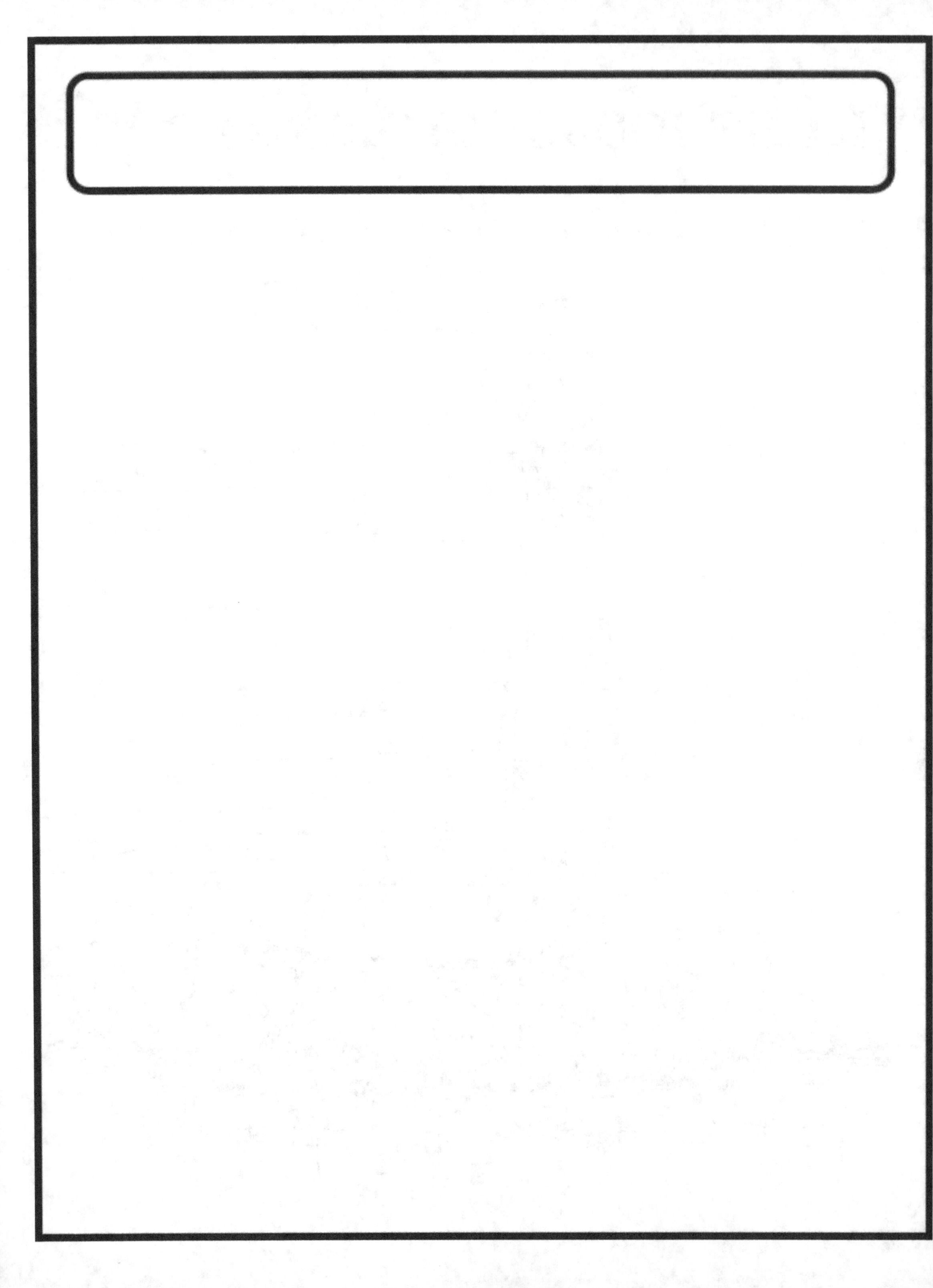

LIGHTHOUSE COLORING BOOK

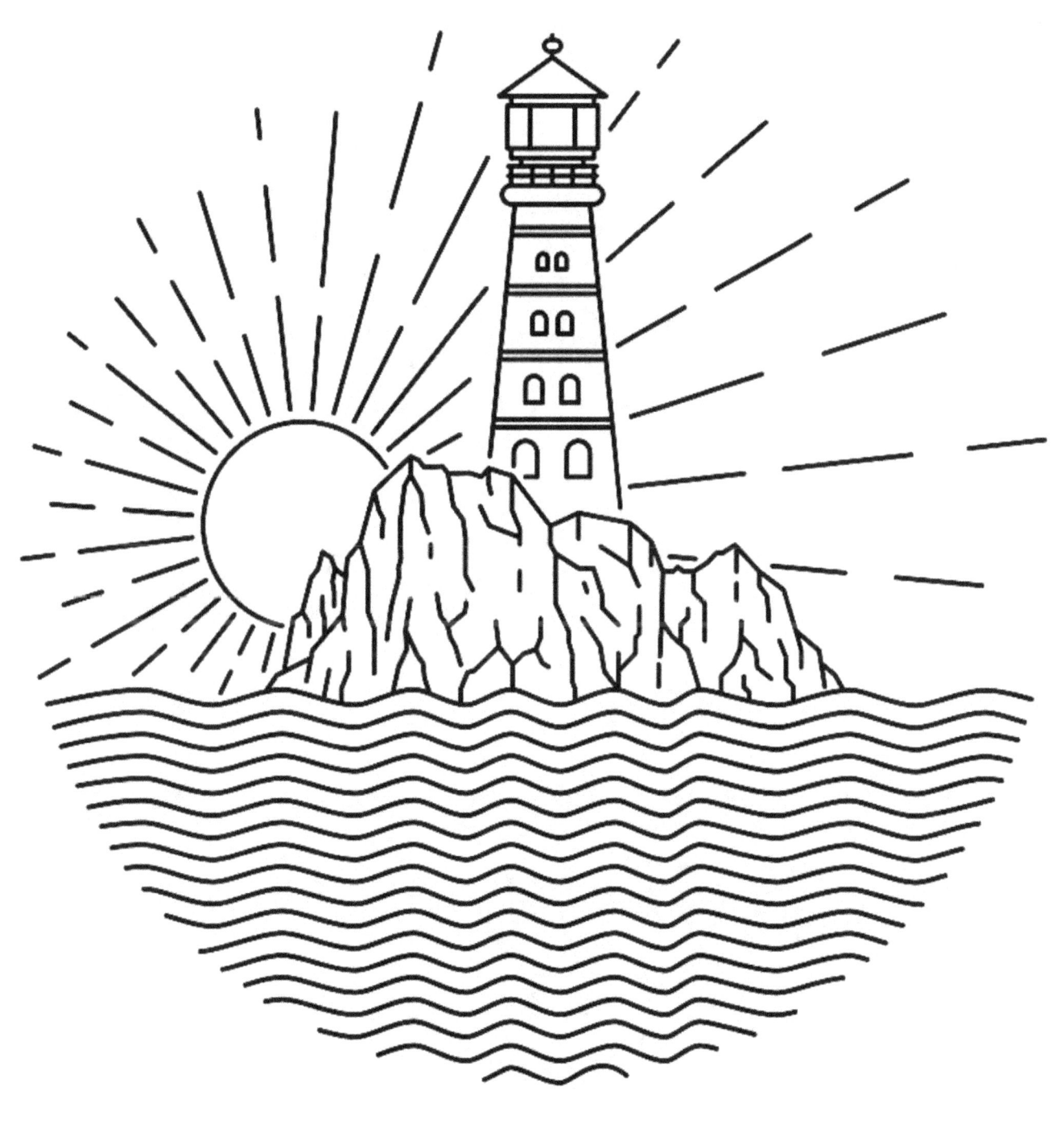

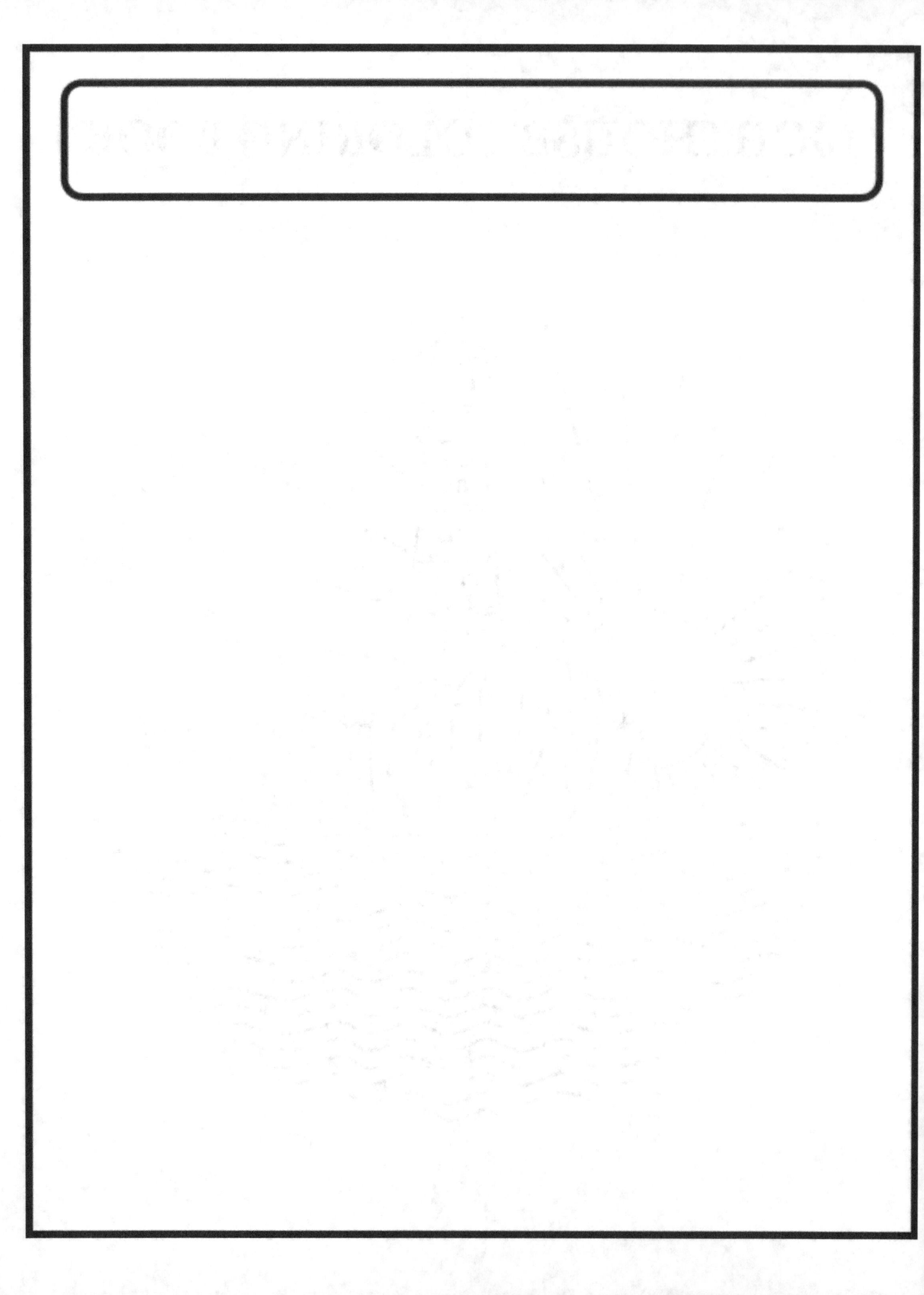

LIGHTHOUSE COLORING BOOK

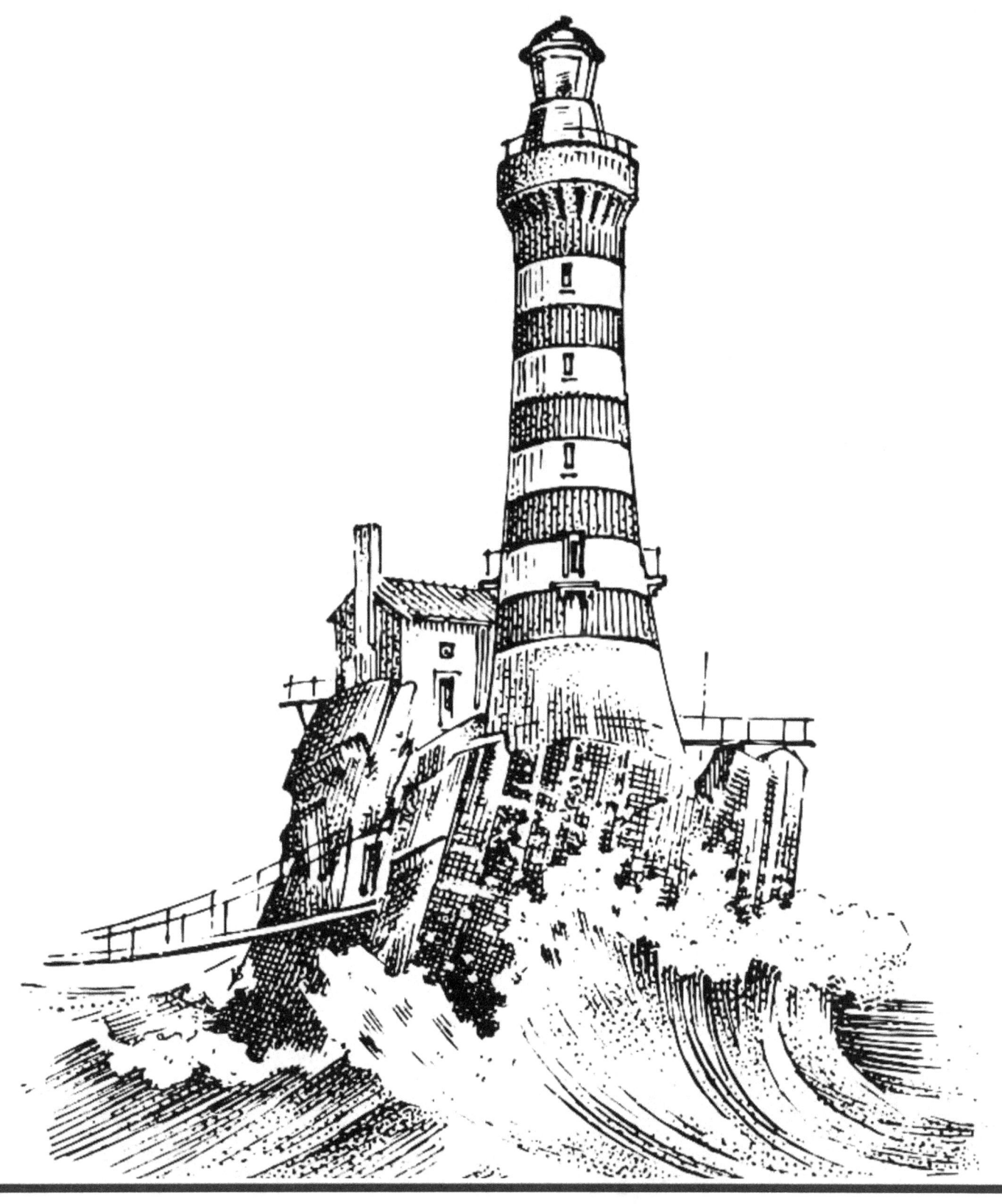

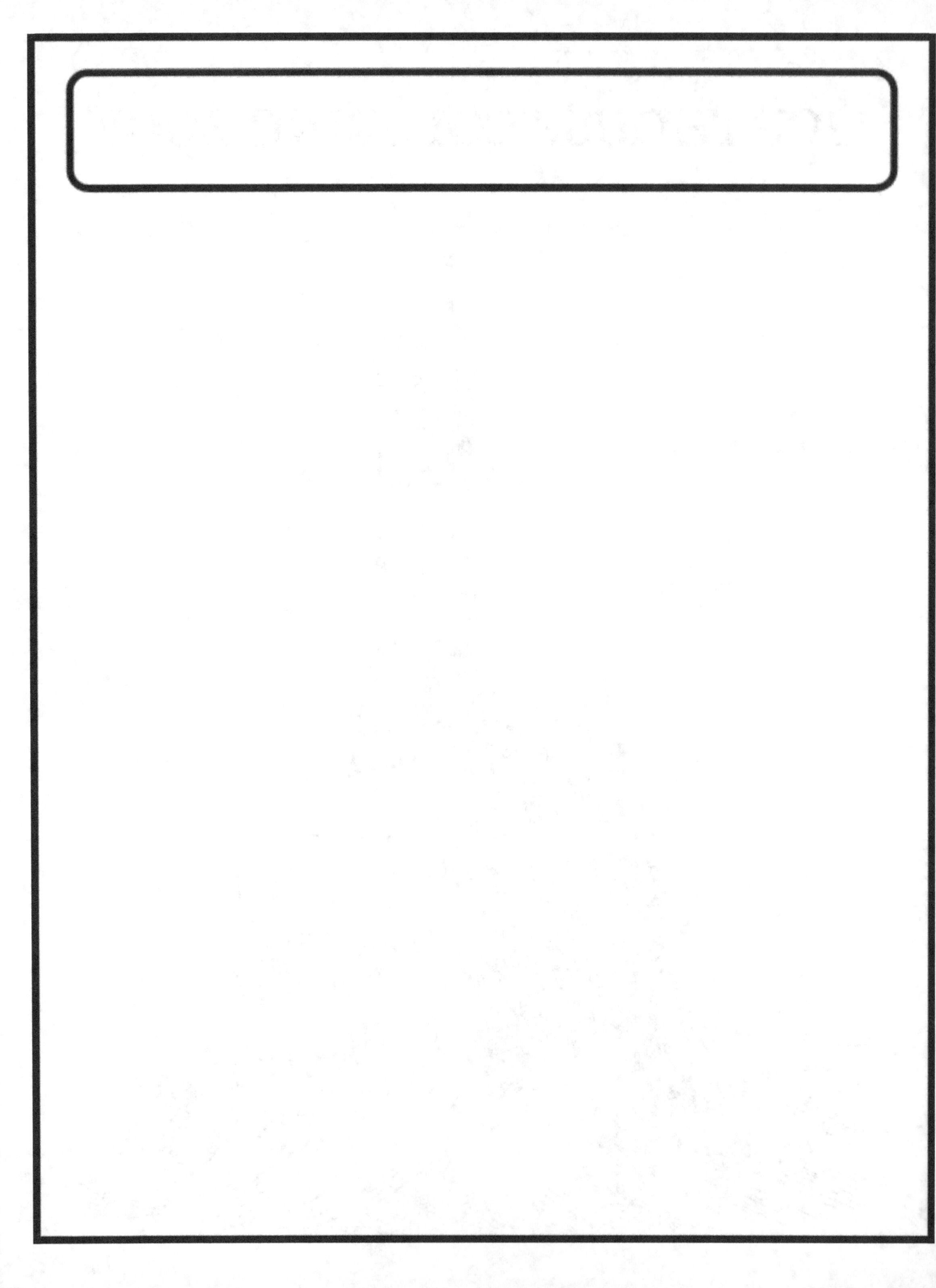

LIGHTHOUSE COLORING BOOK

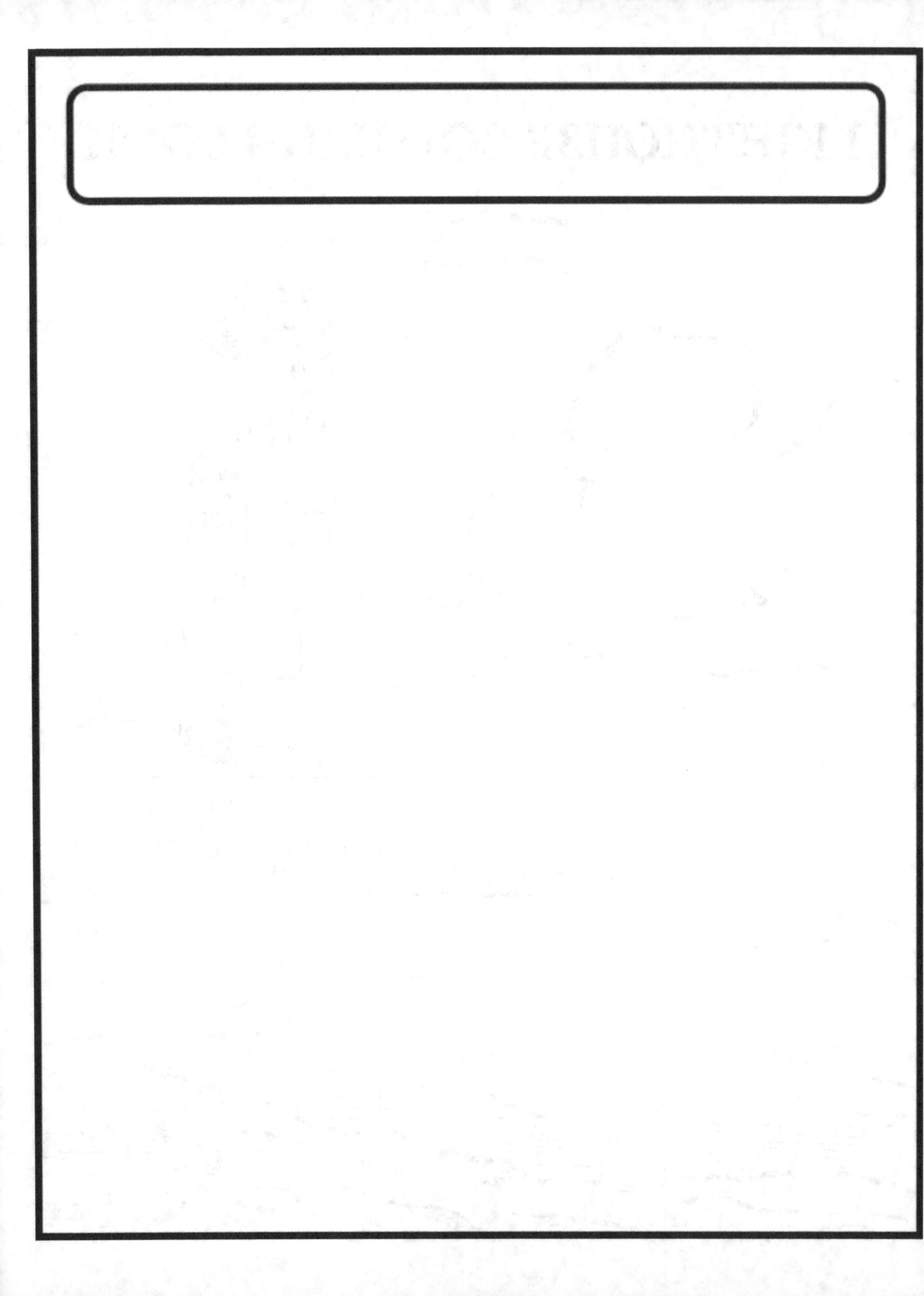

LIGHTHOUSE COLORING BOOK

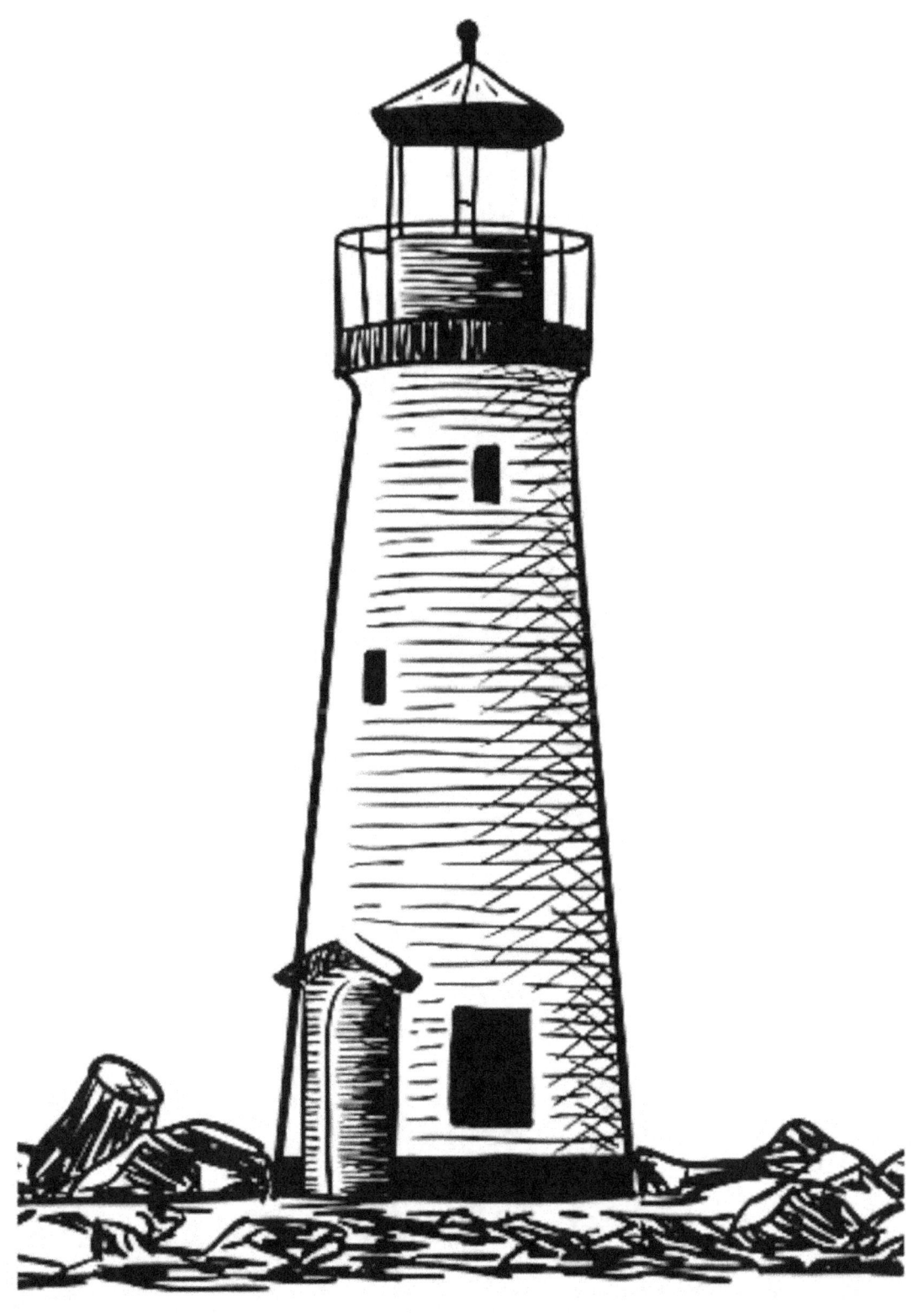

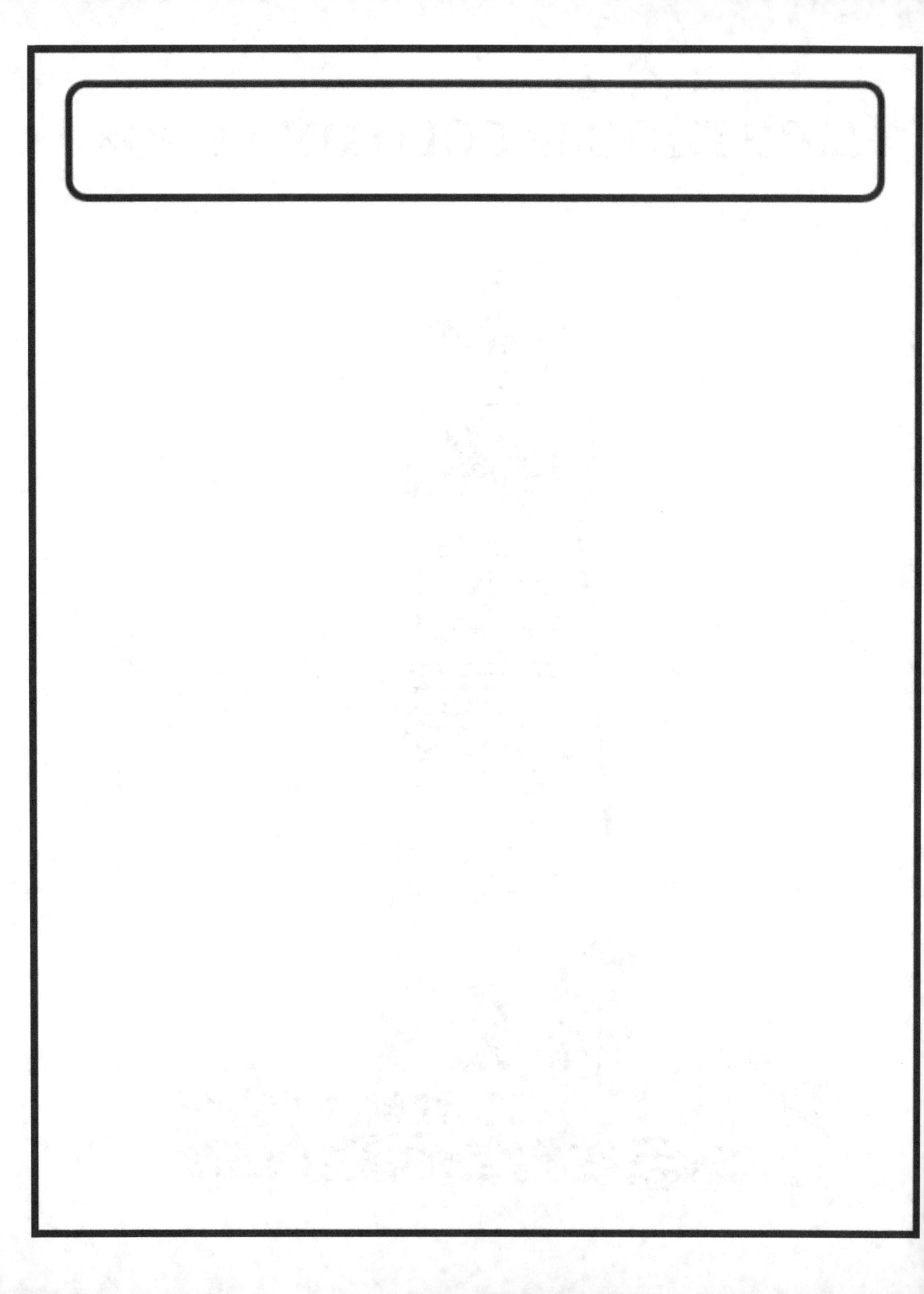

LIGHTHOUSE COLORING BOOK

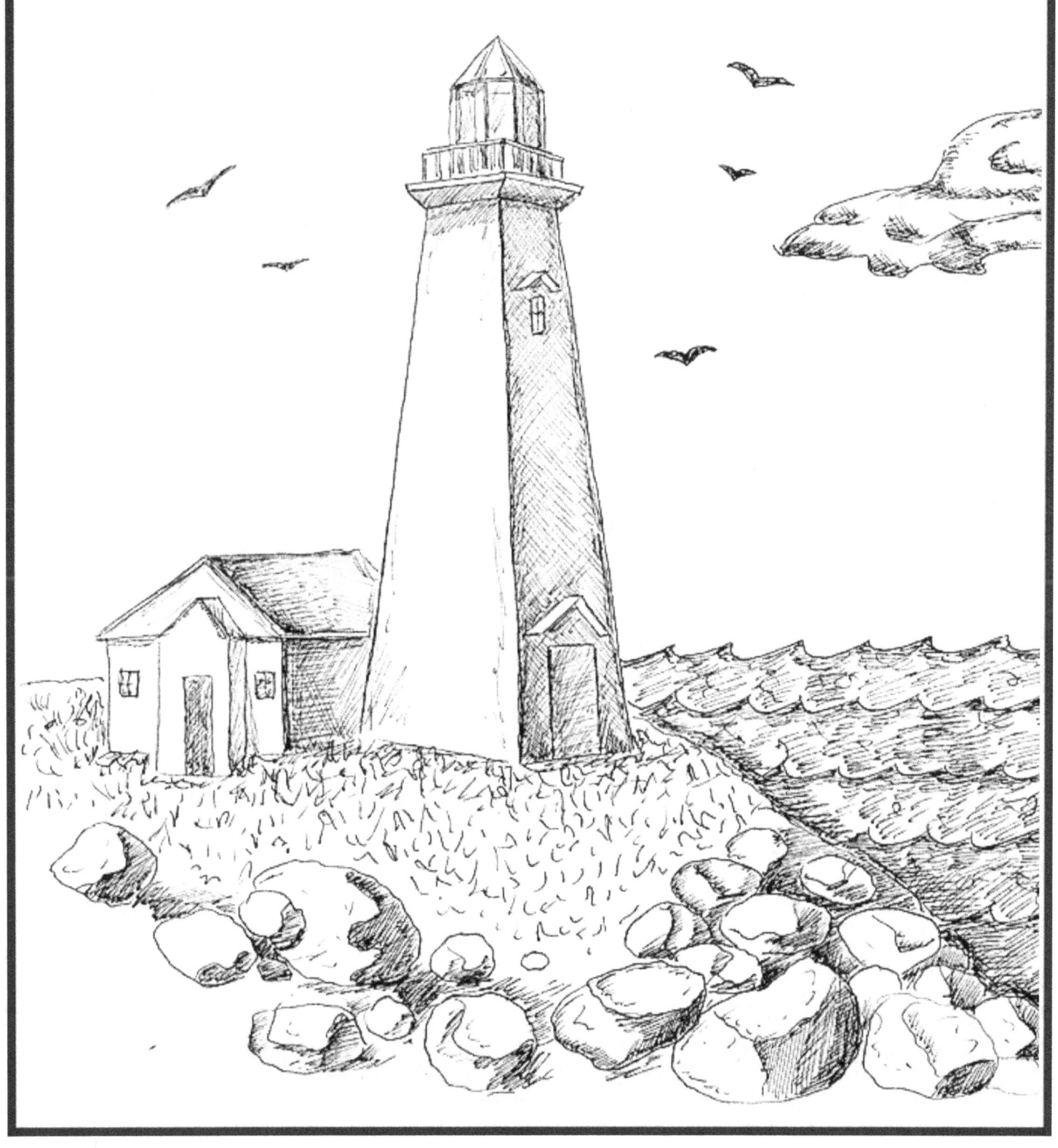

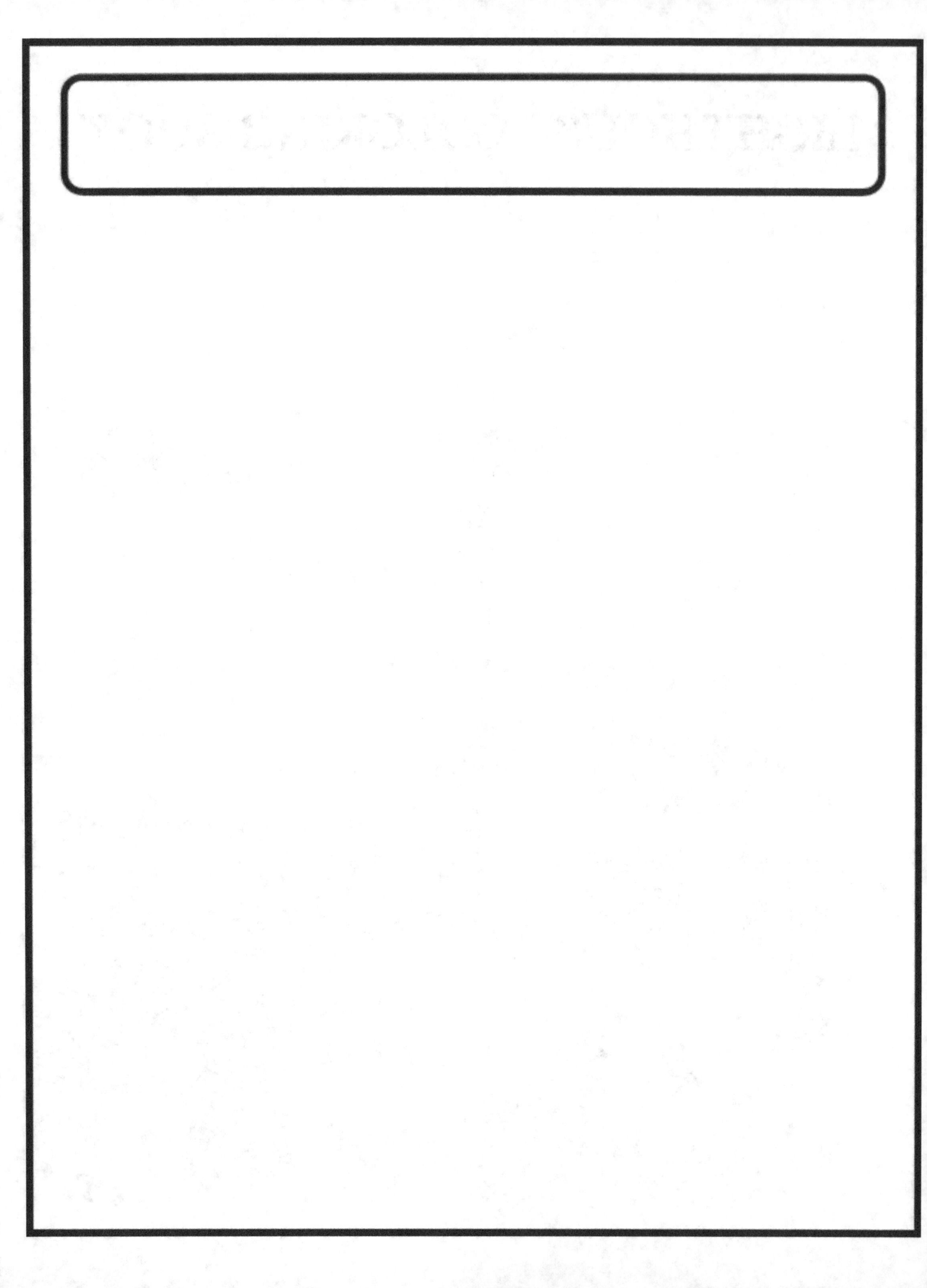

LIGHTHOUSE COLORING BOOK

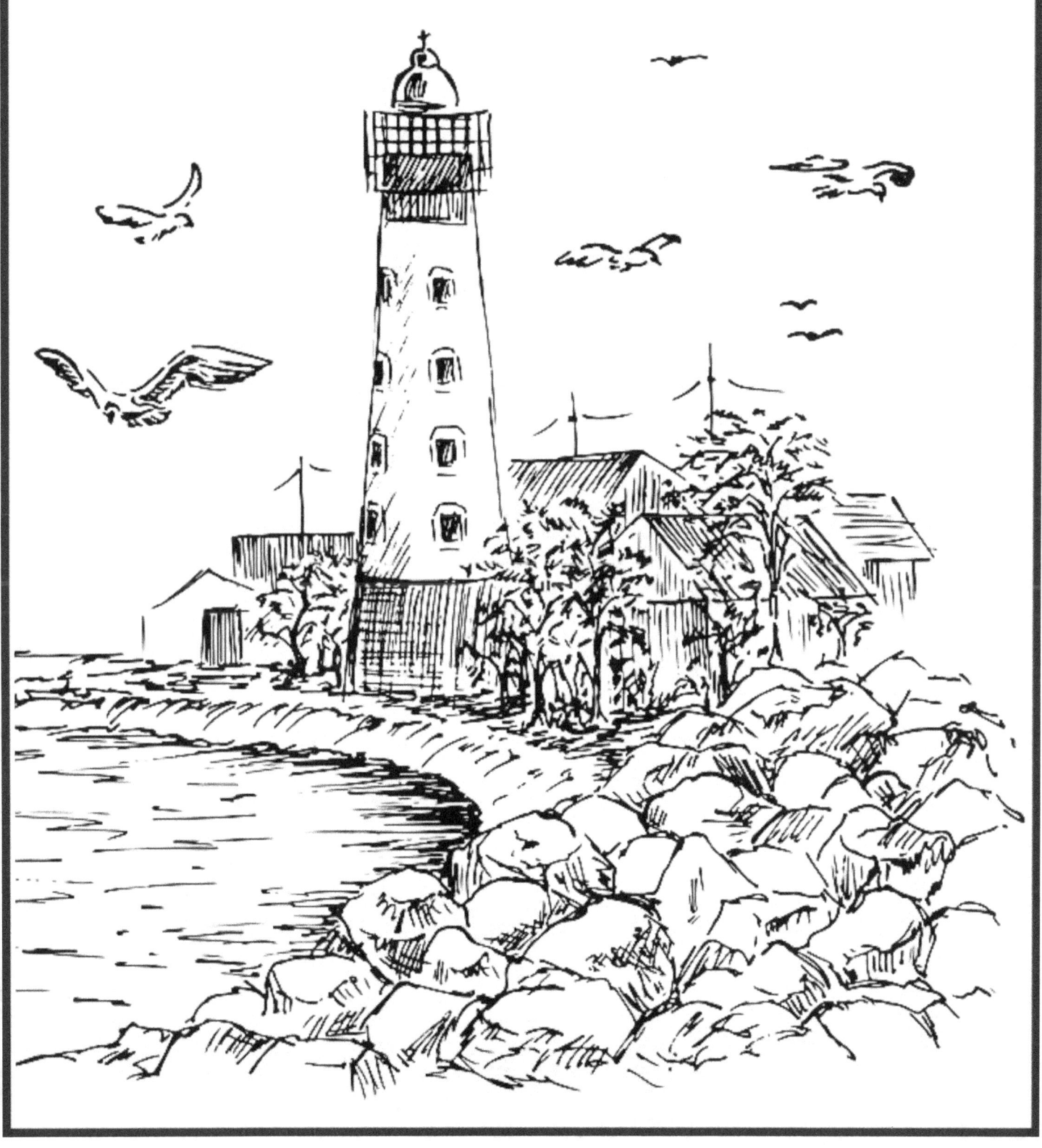

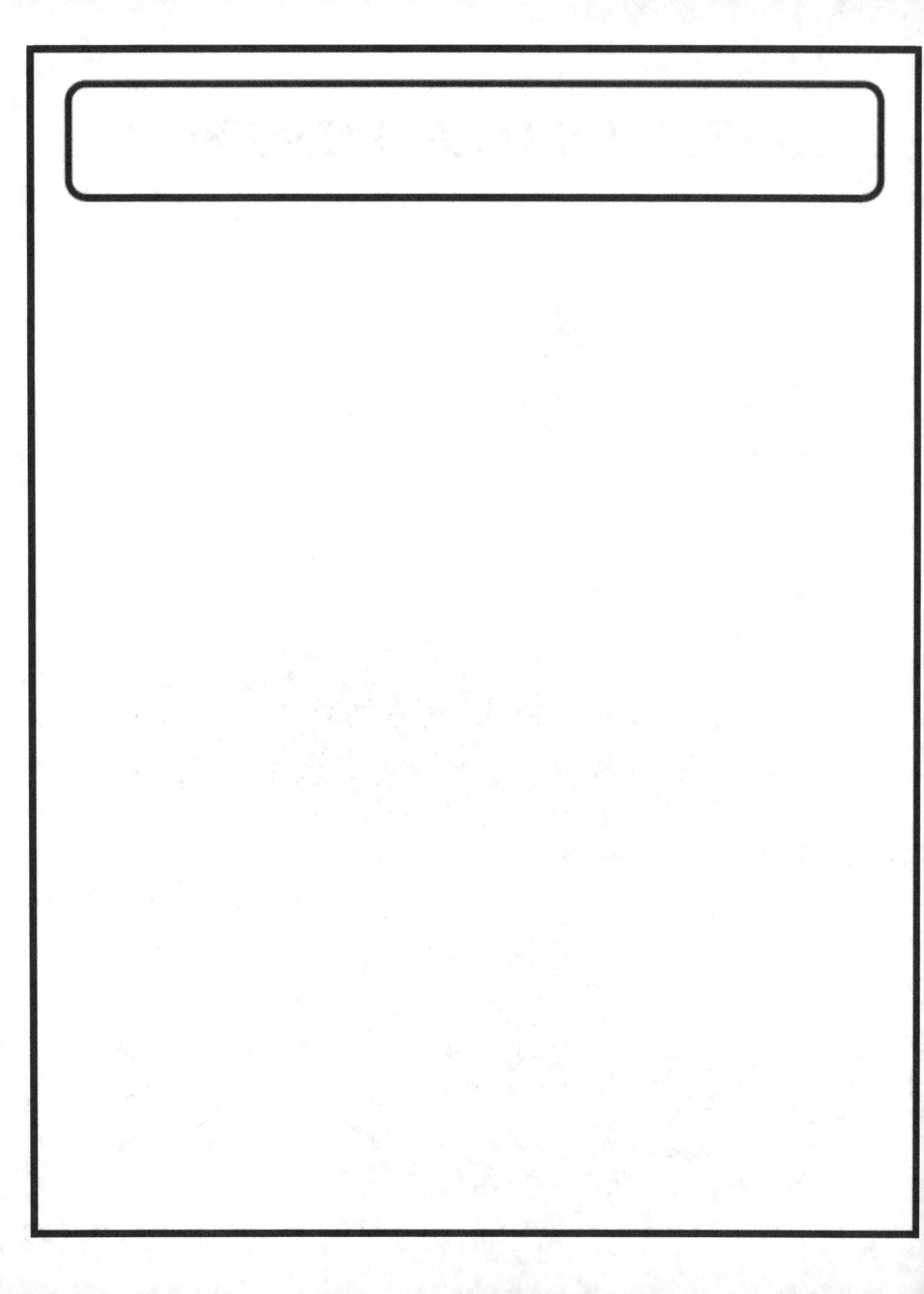

LIGHTHOUSE COLORING BOOK

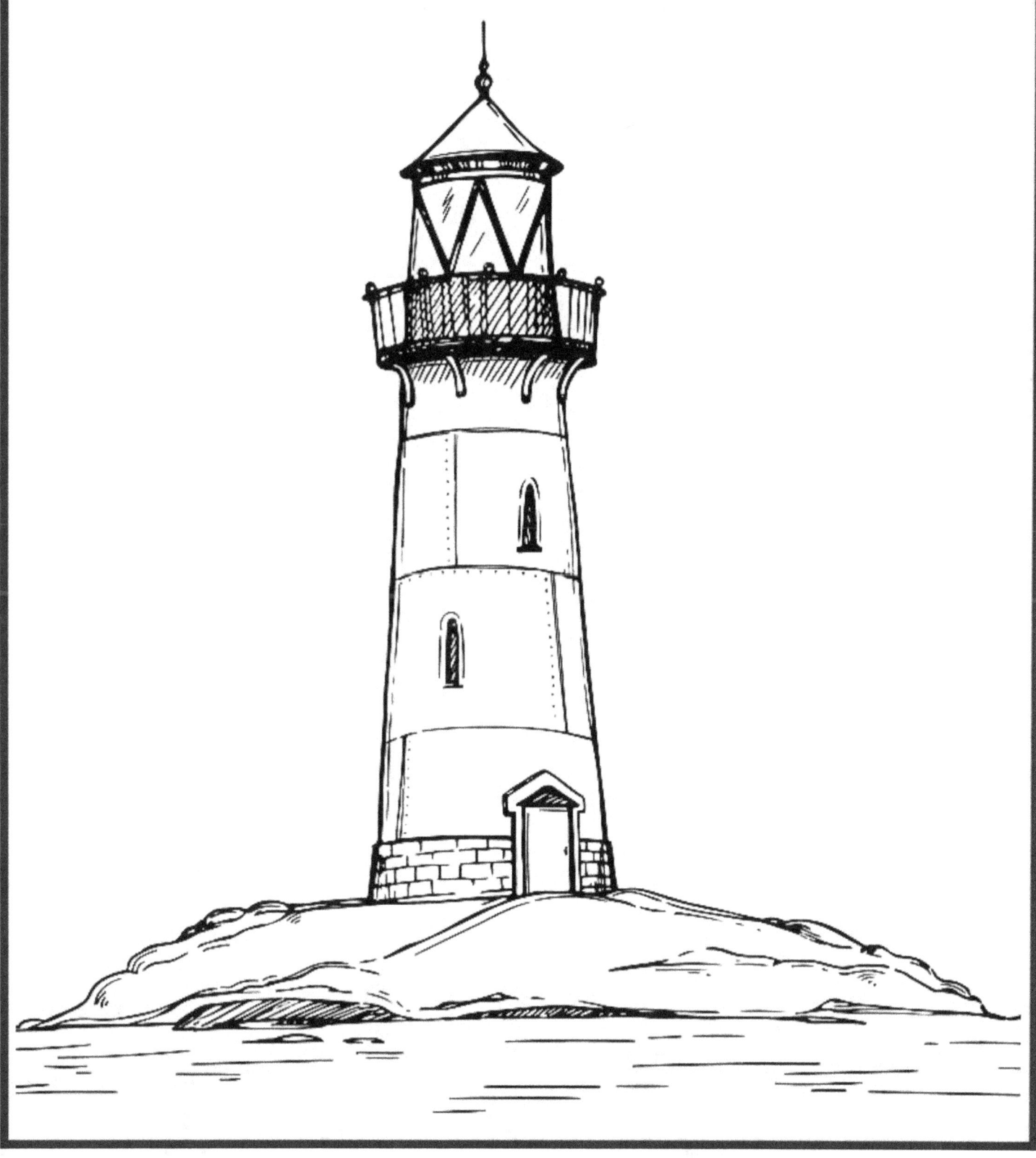

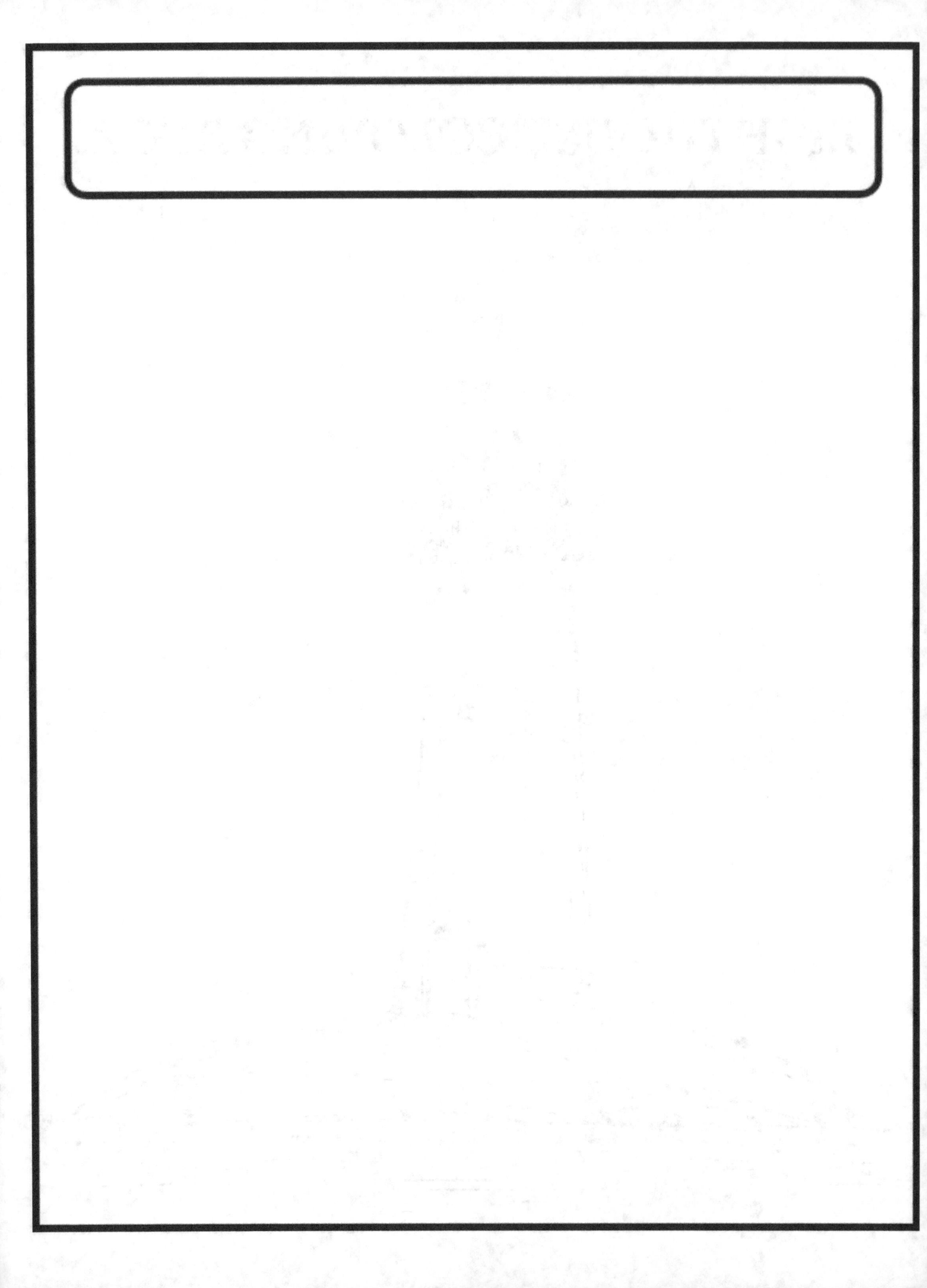

LIGHTHOUSE COLORING BOOK

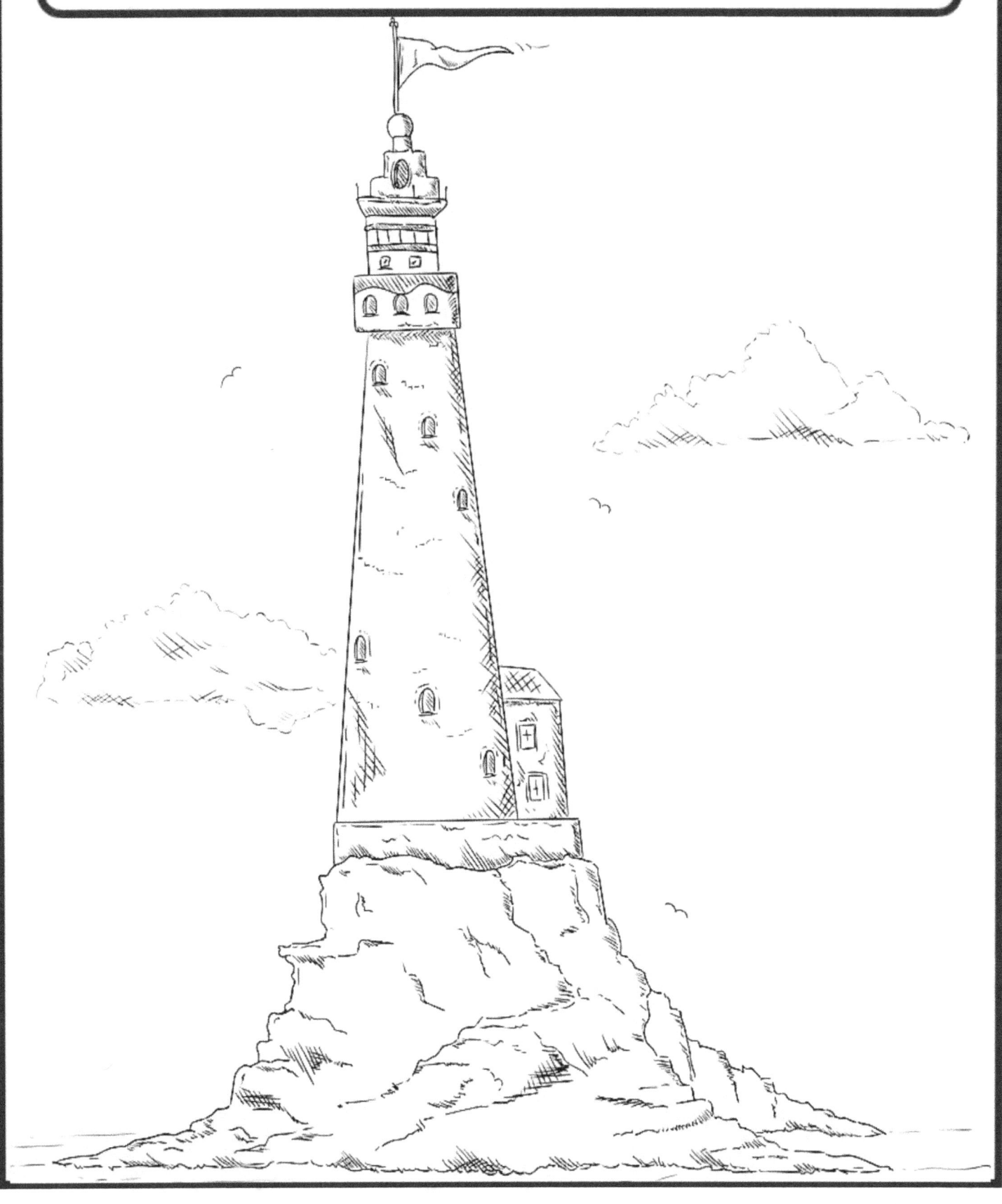

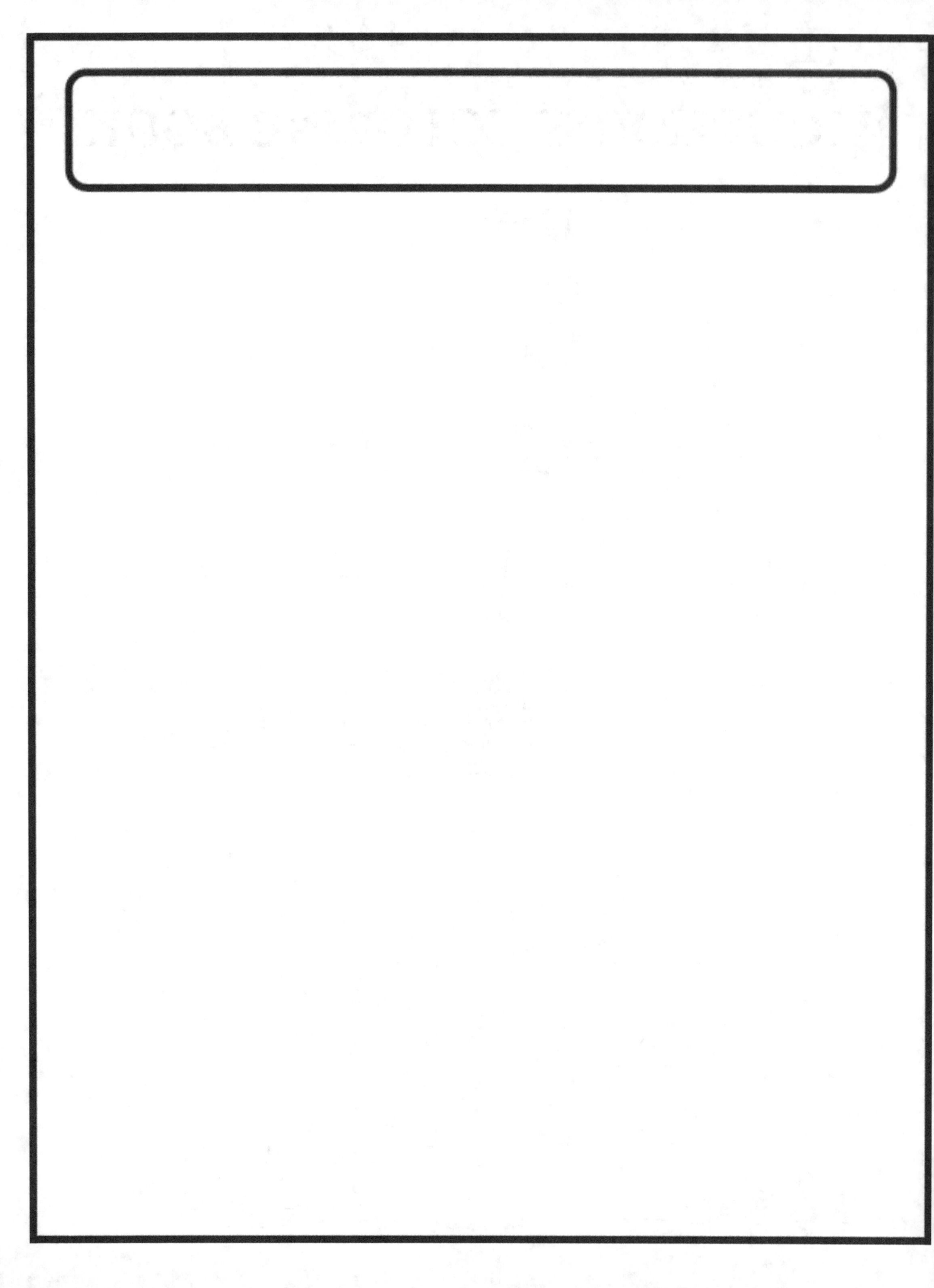

LIGHTHOUSE COLORING BOOK

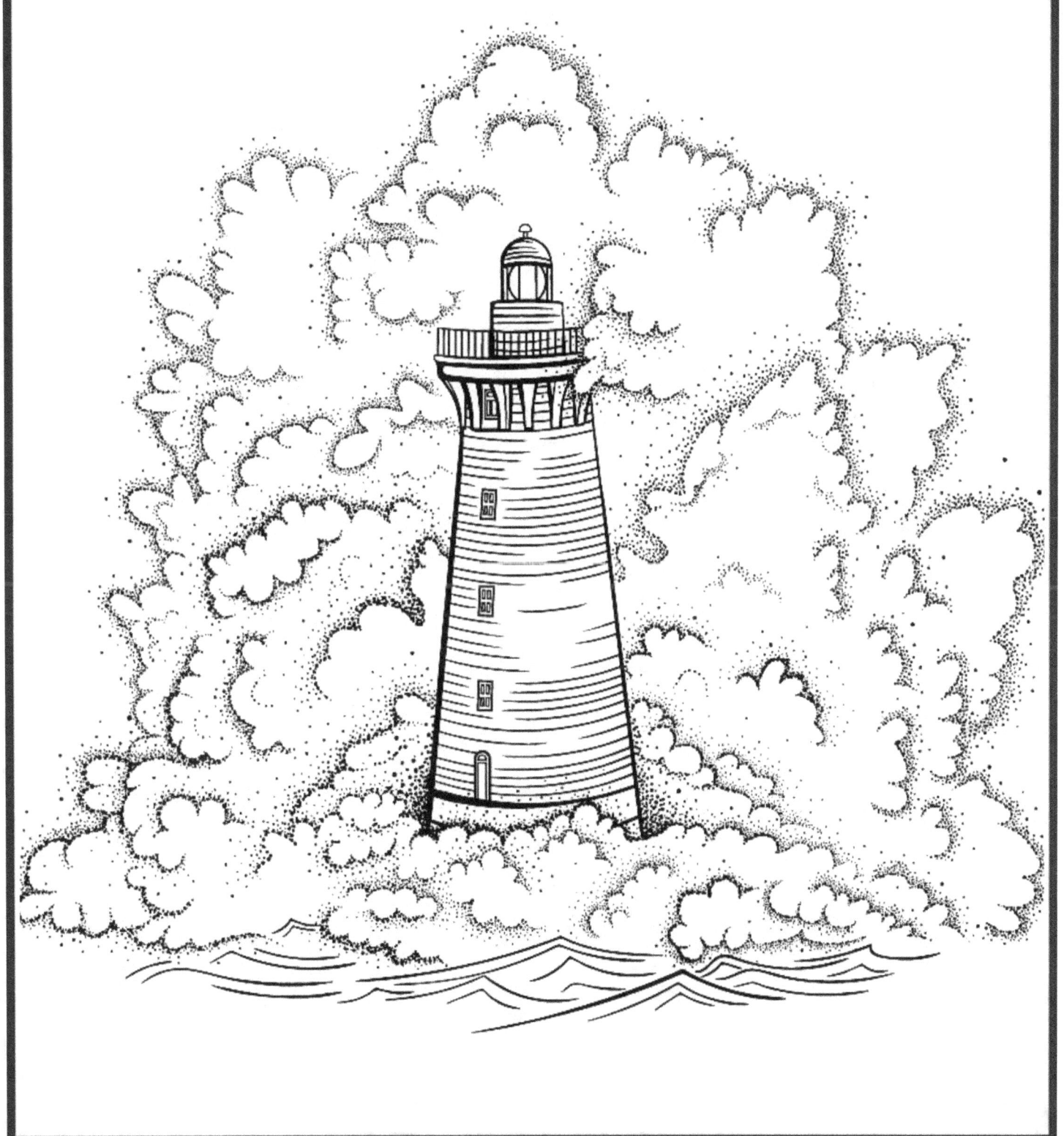

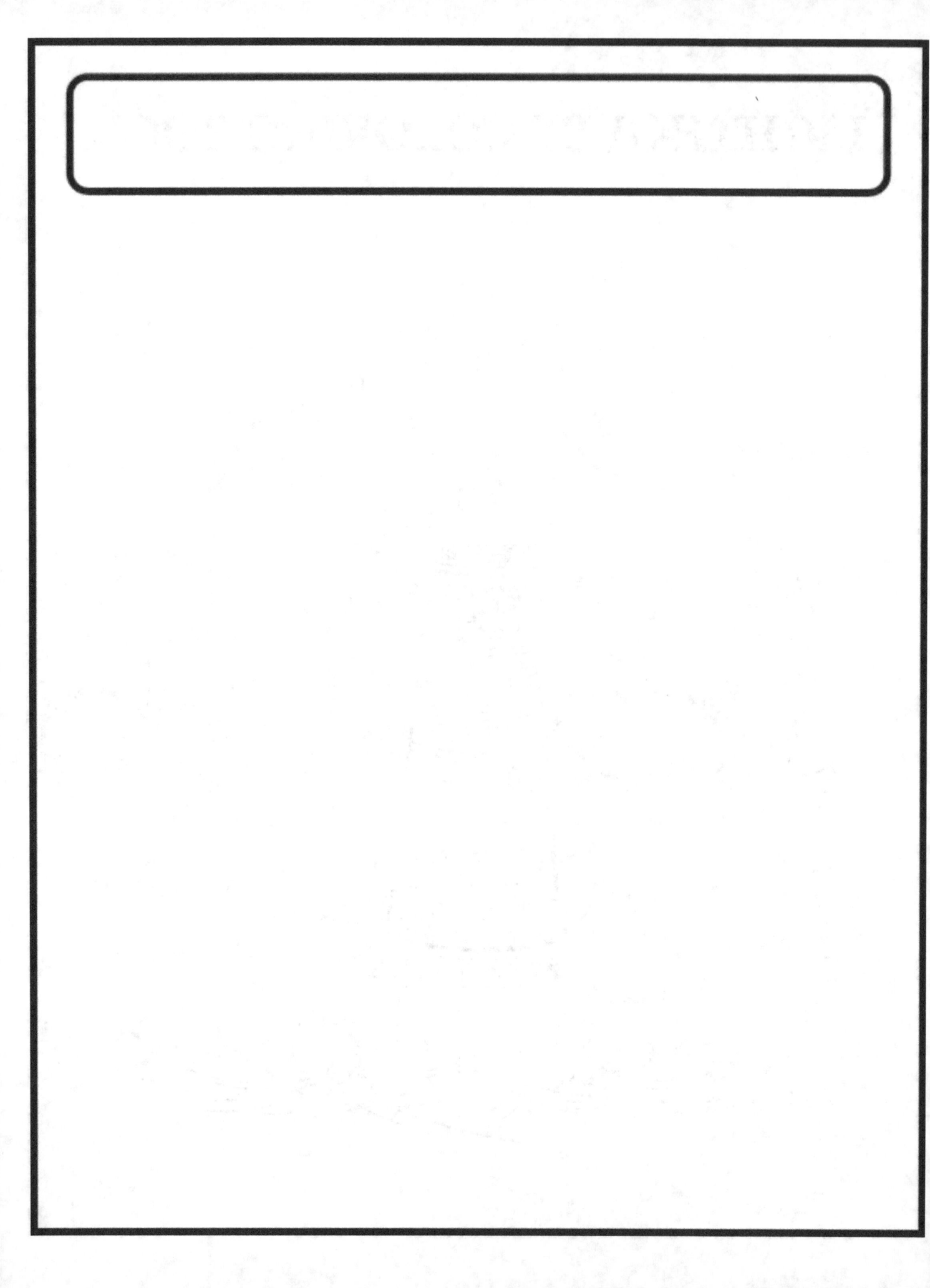

LIGHTHOUSE COLORING BOOK

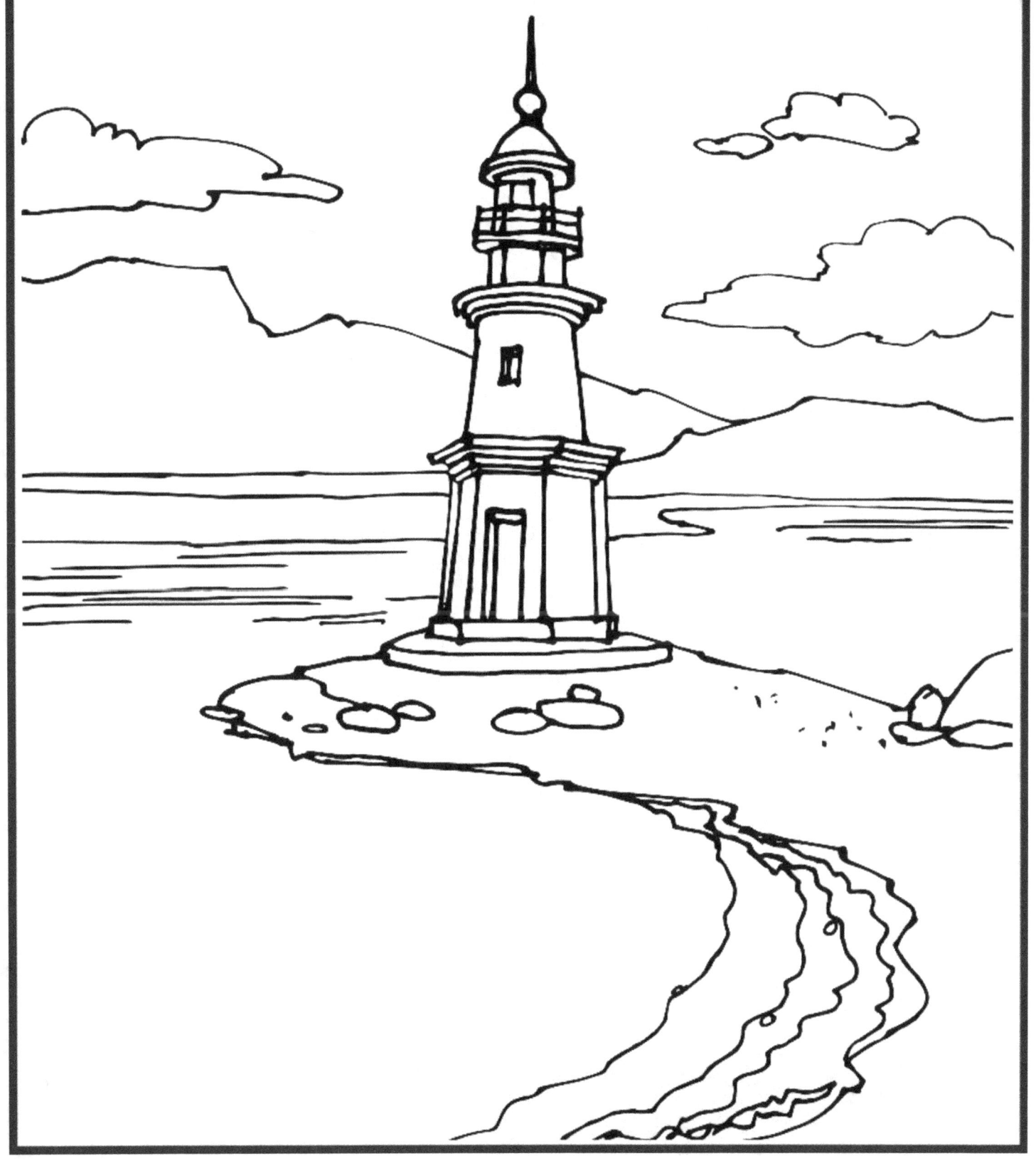

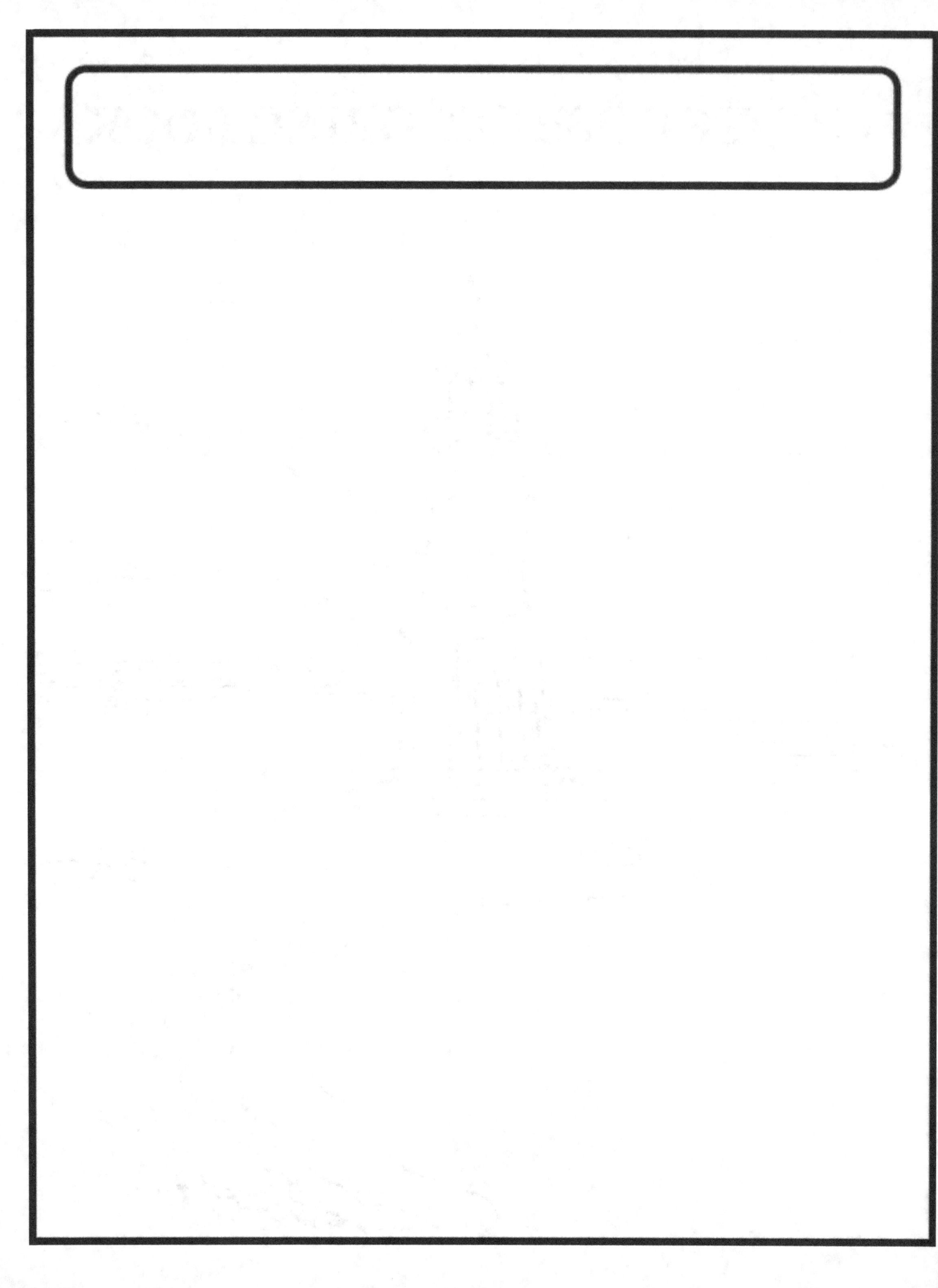

LIGHTHOUSE COLORING BOOK

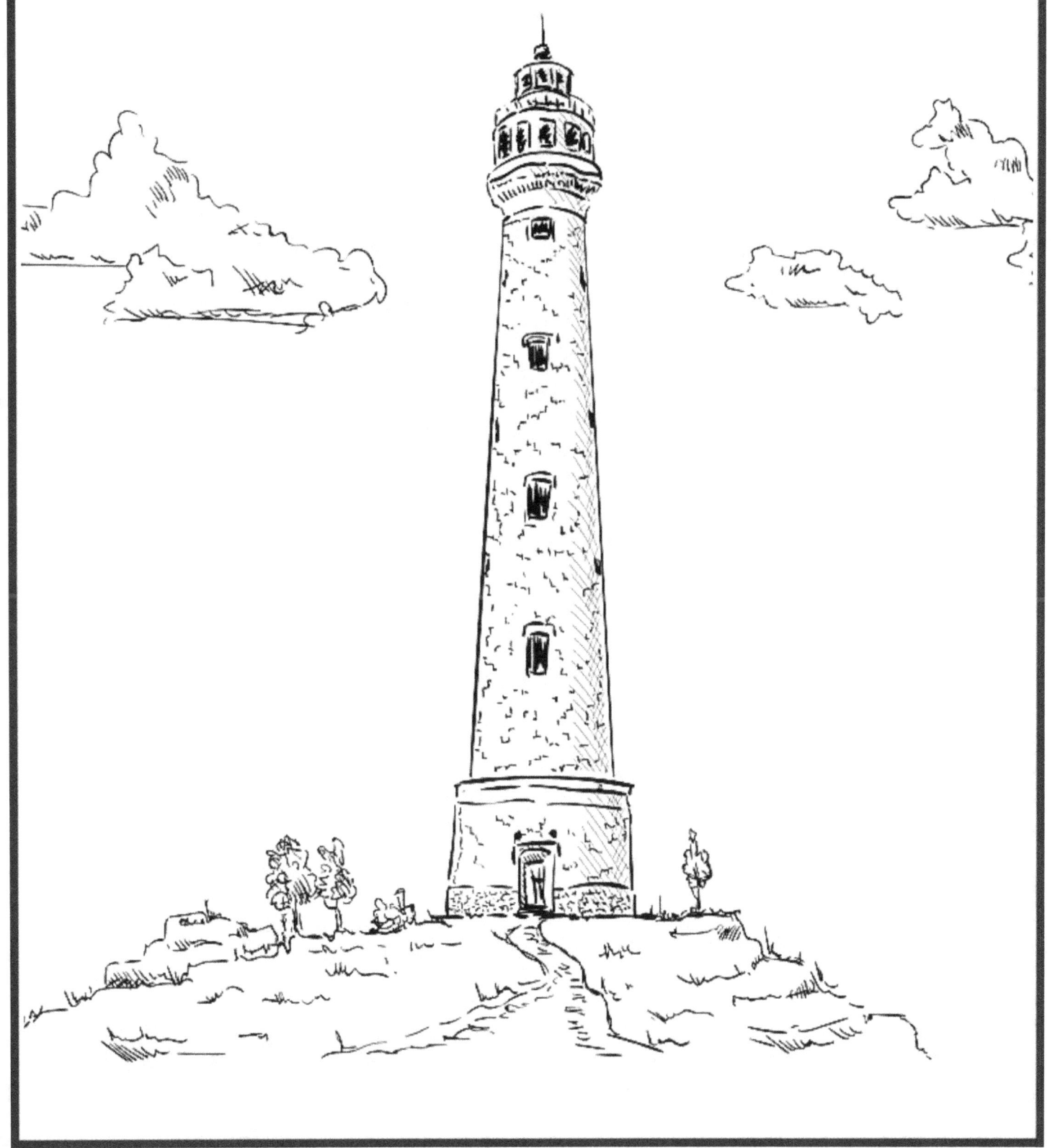

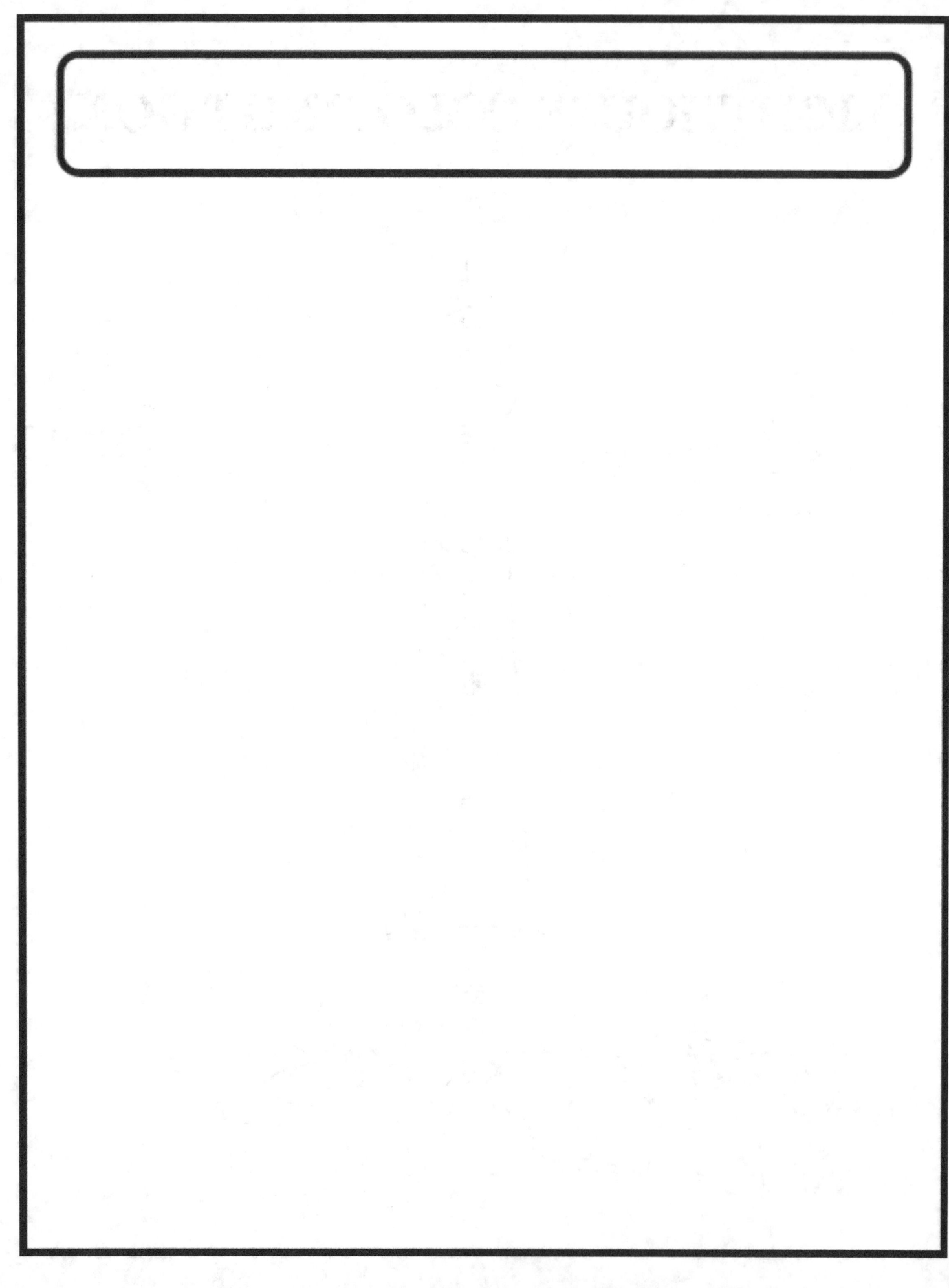

LIGHTHOUSE COLORING BOOK

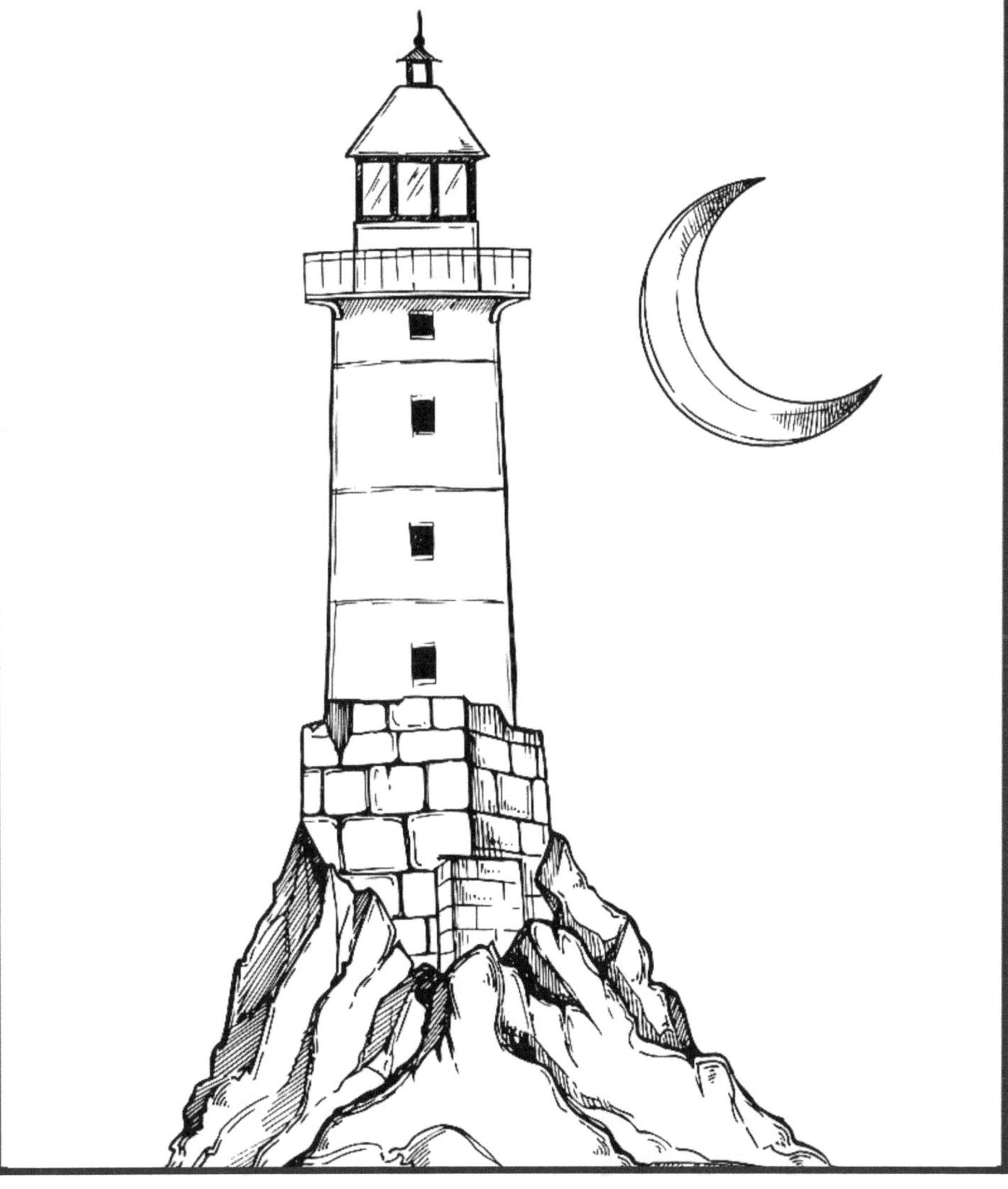

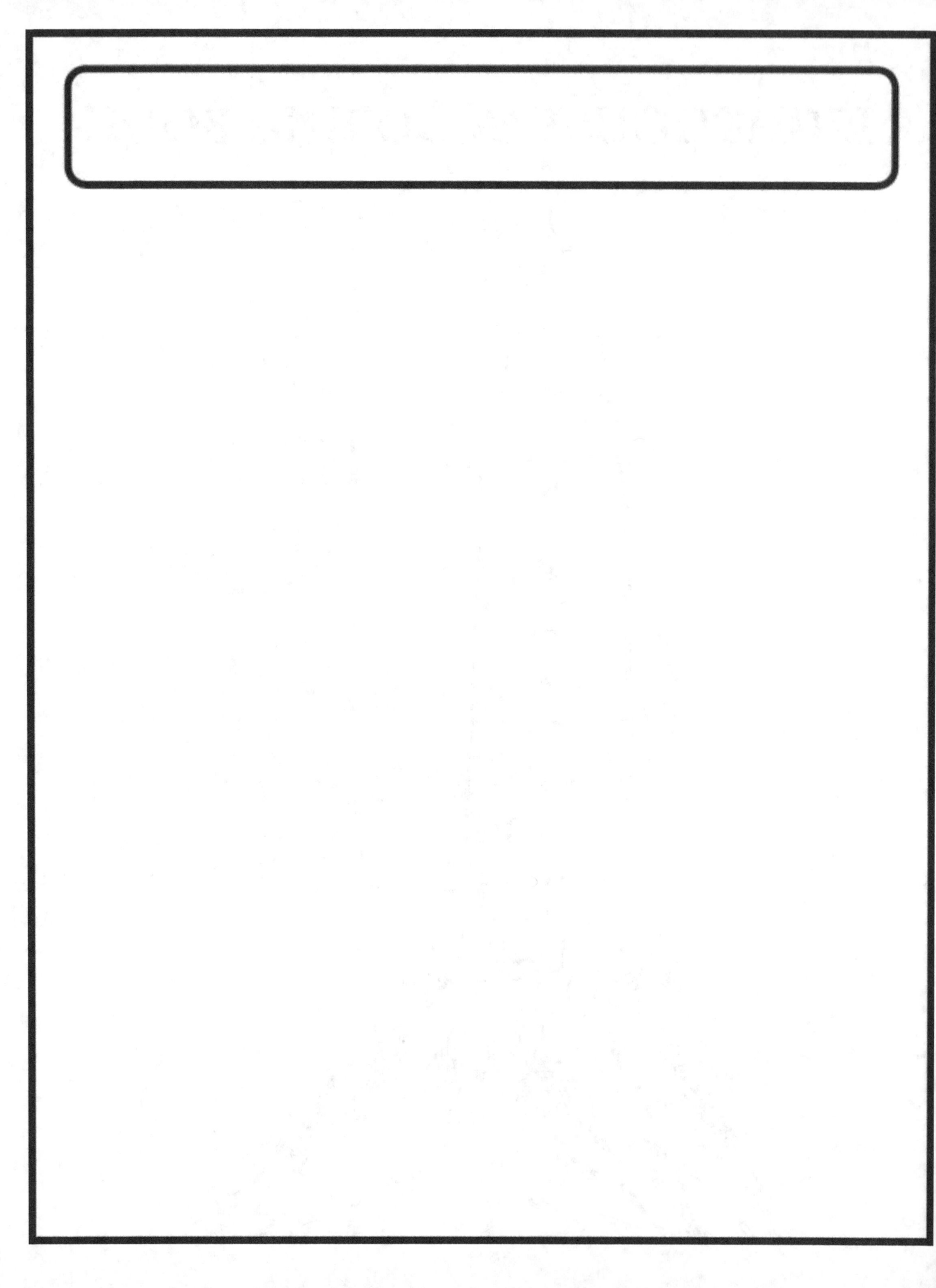

LIGHTHOUSE COLORING BOOK

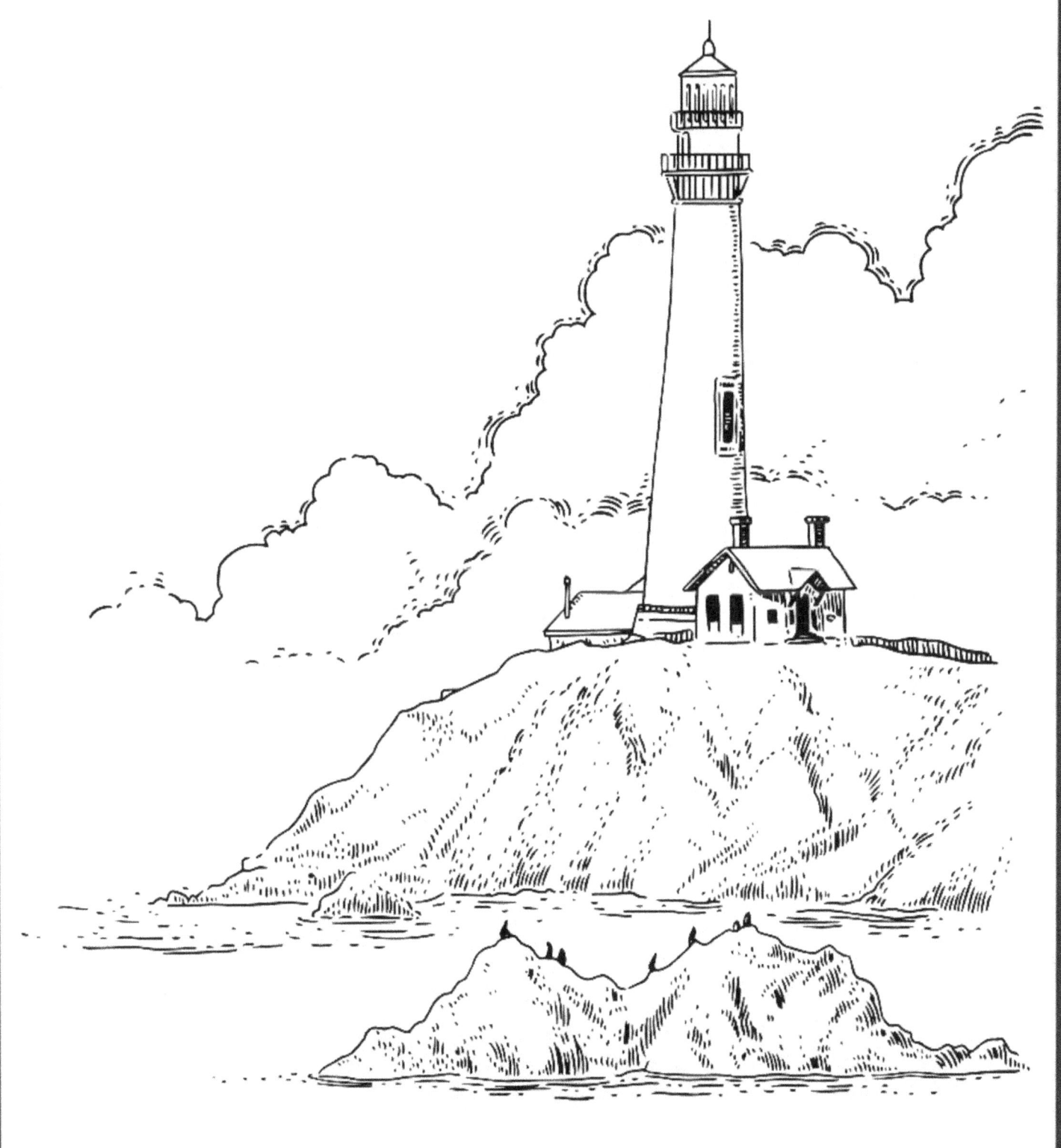

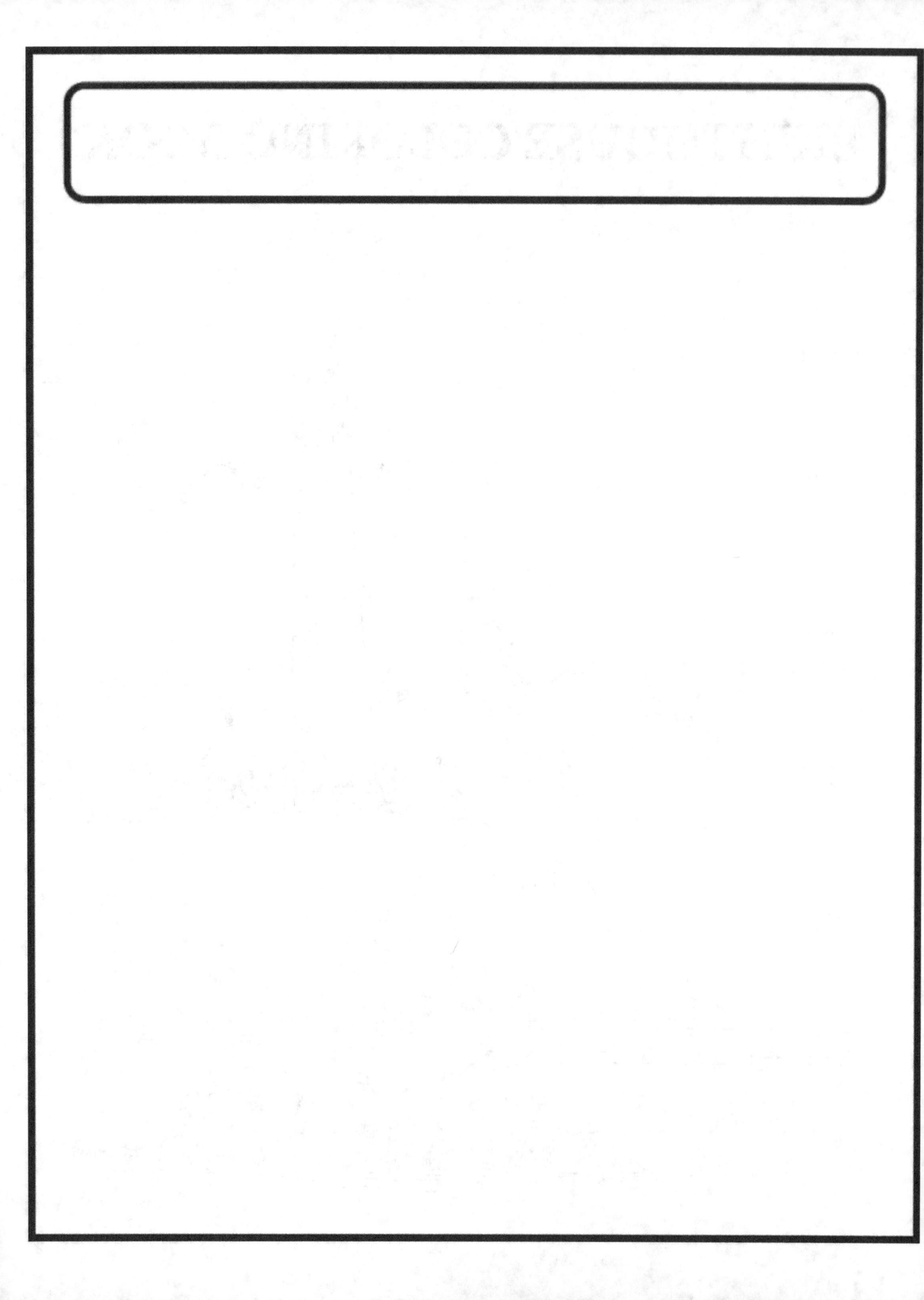

LIGHTHOUSE COLORING BOOK

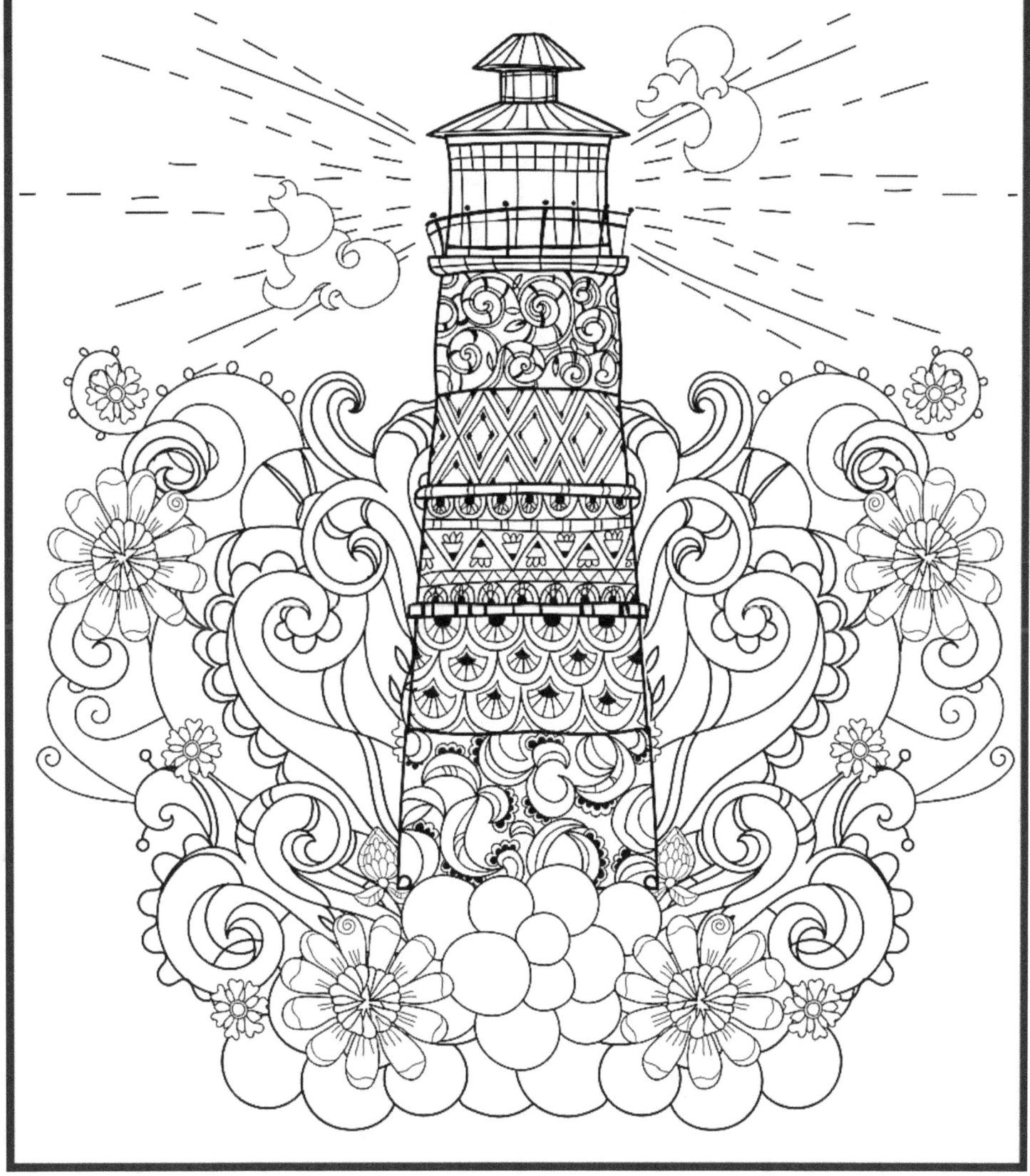

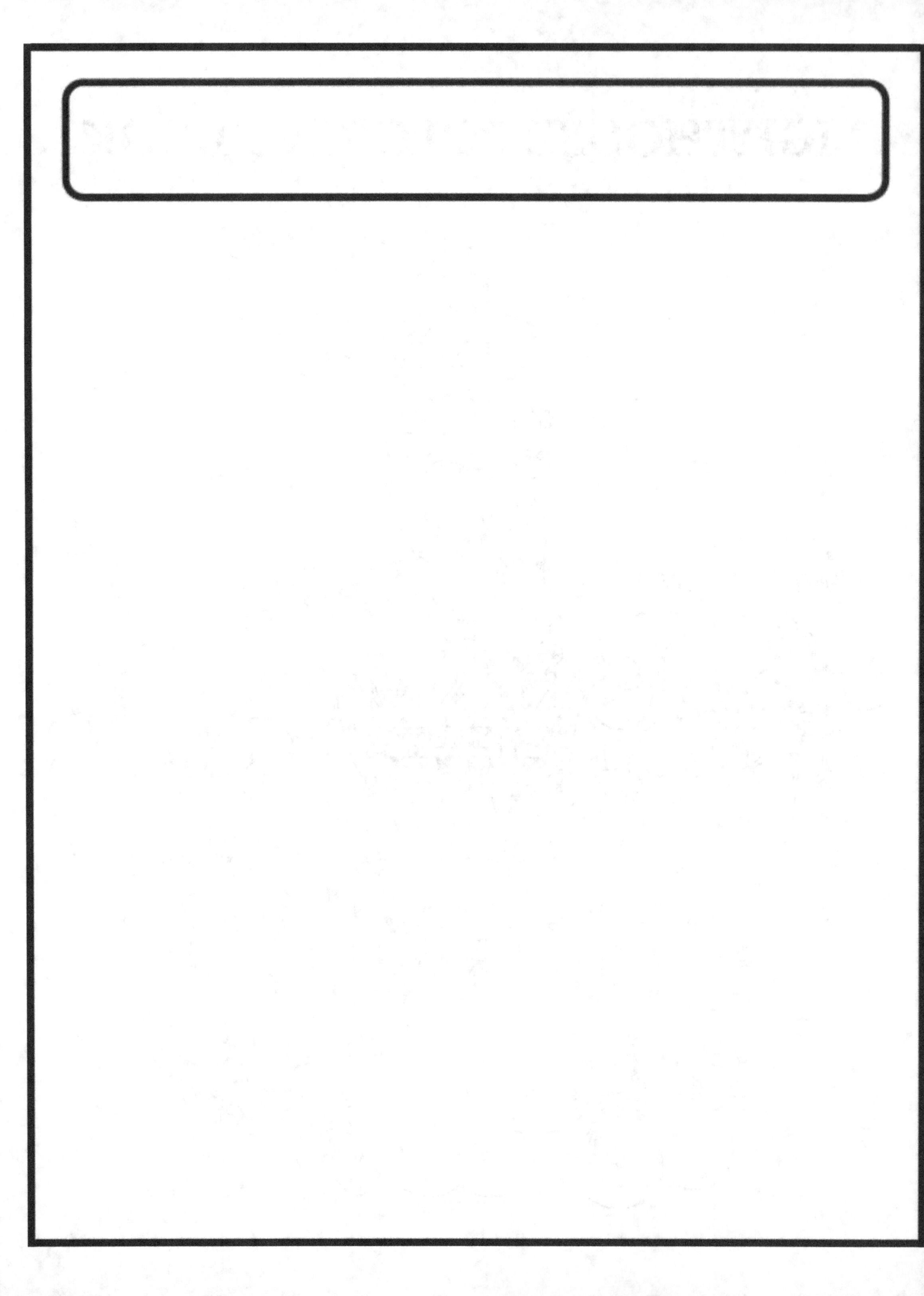

LIGHTHOUSE COLORING BOOK

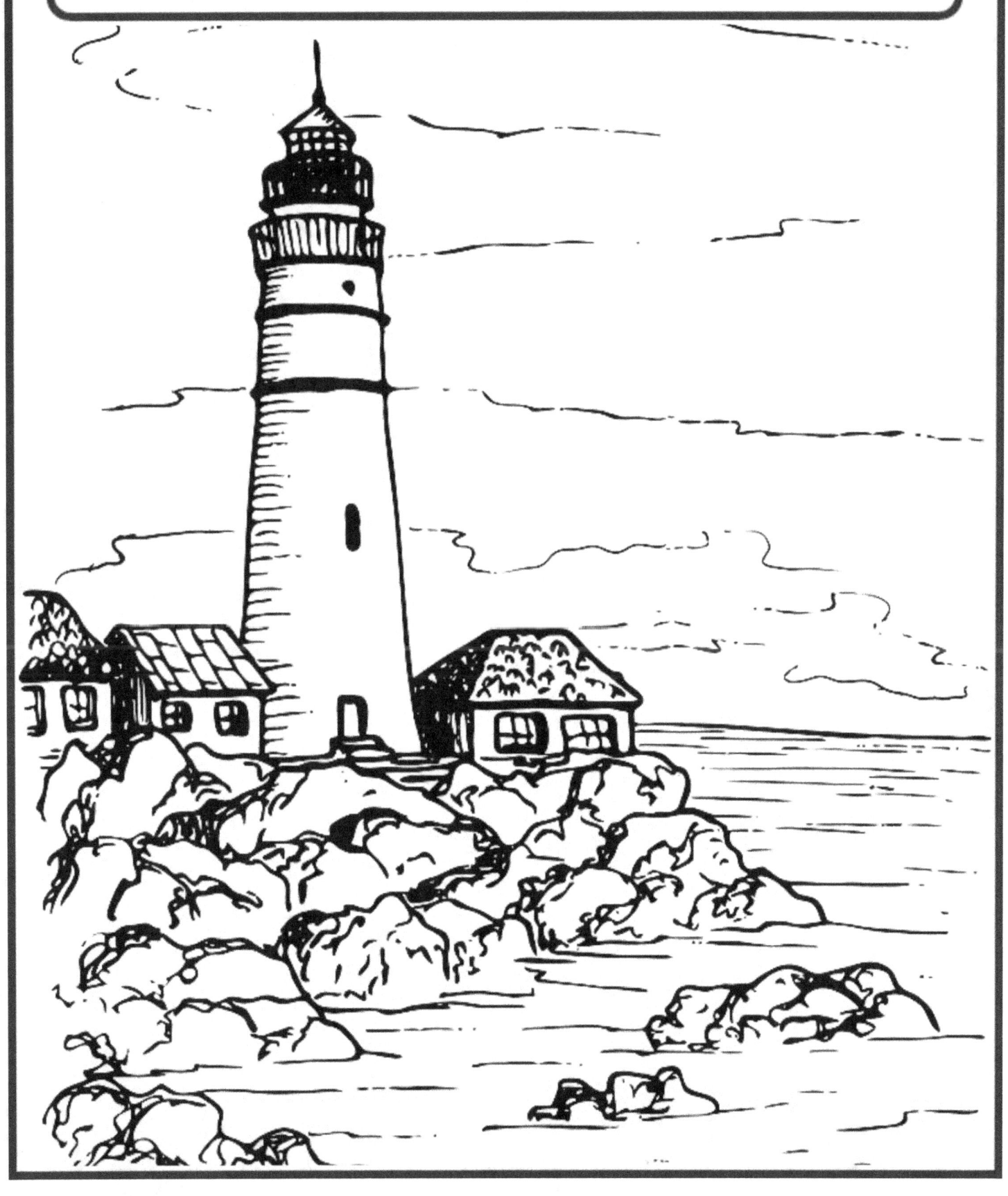

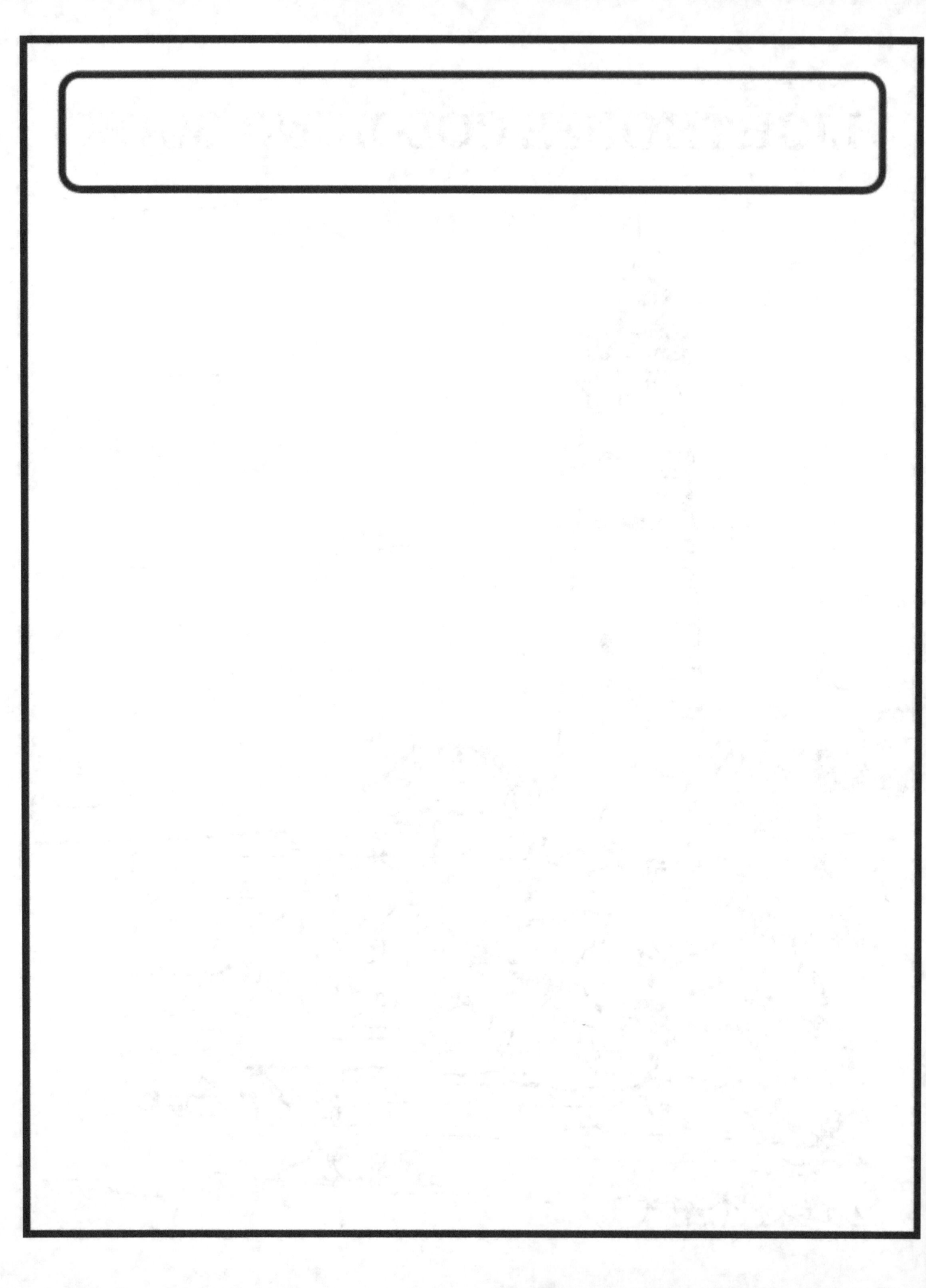

LIGHTHOUSE COLORING BOOK

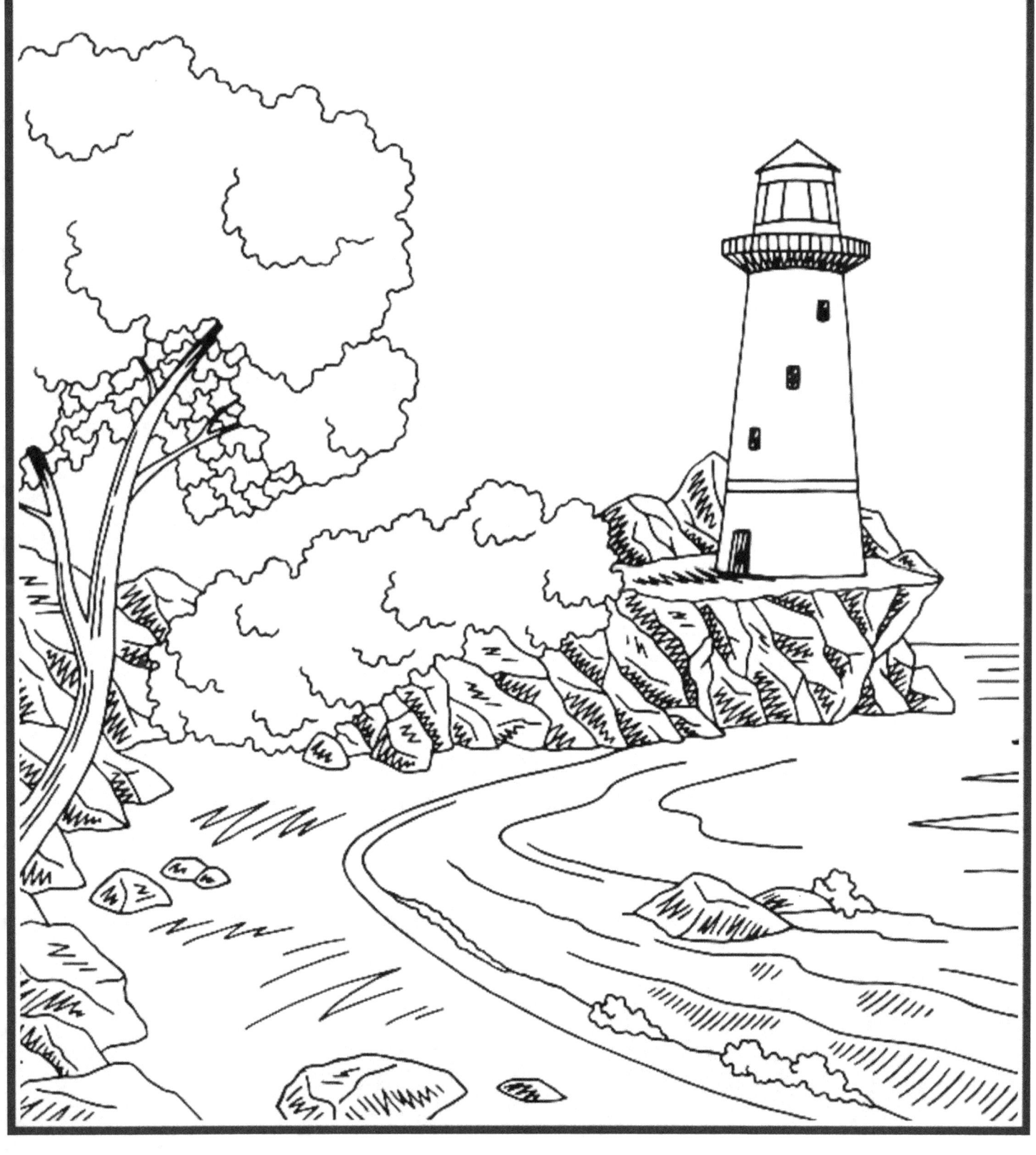

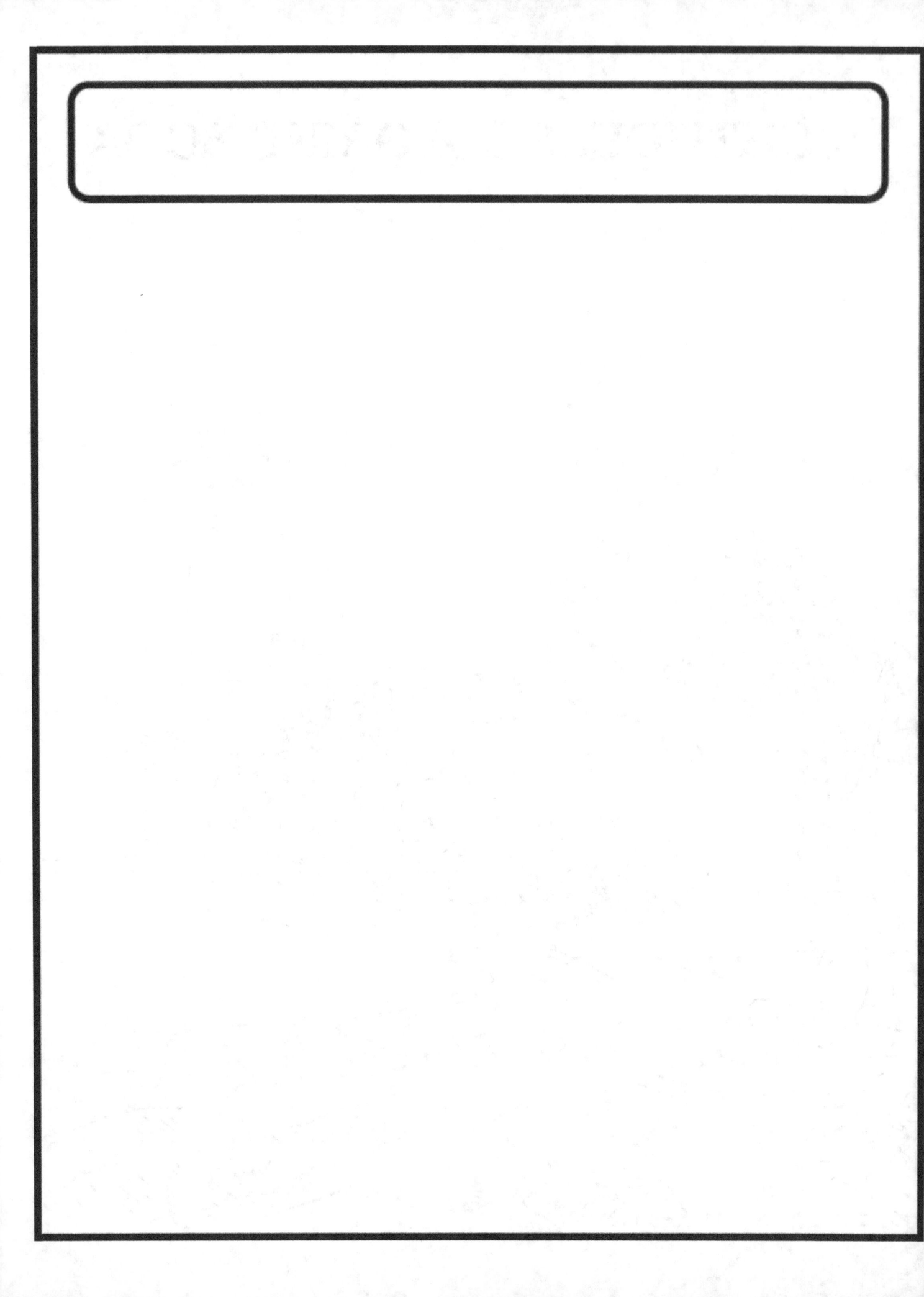

LIGHTHOUSE COLORING BOOK

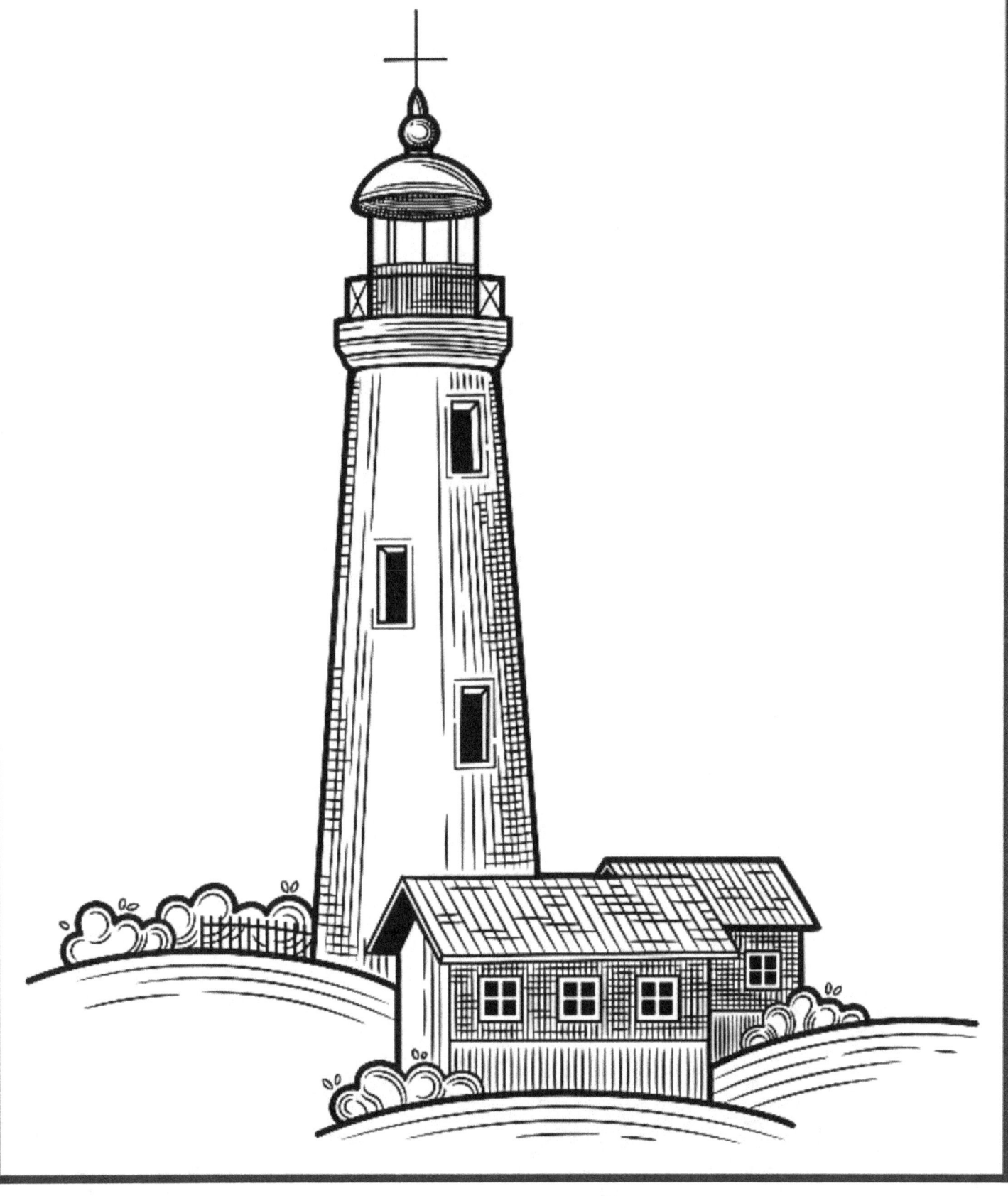

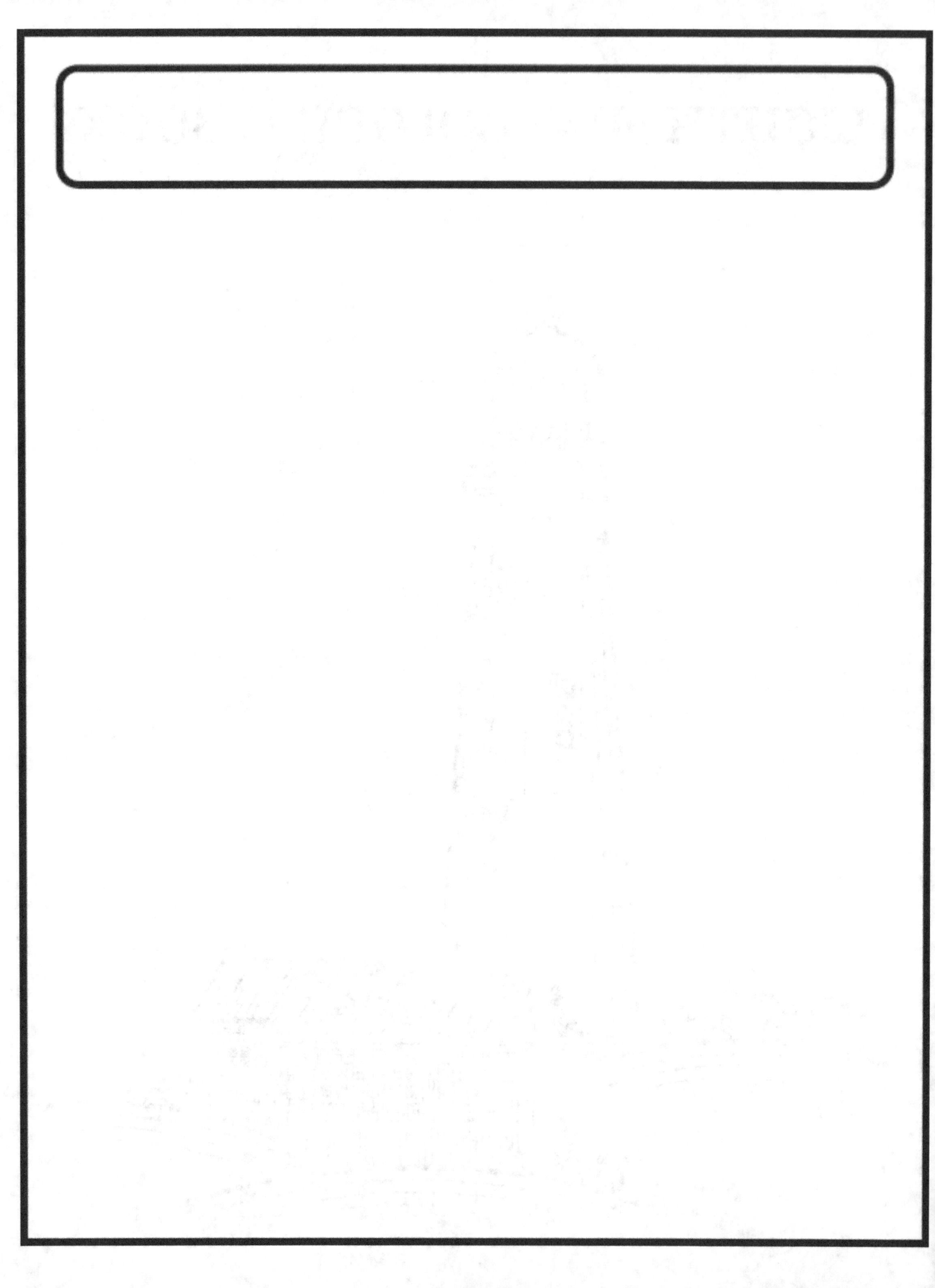

LIGHTHOUSE COLORING BOOK

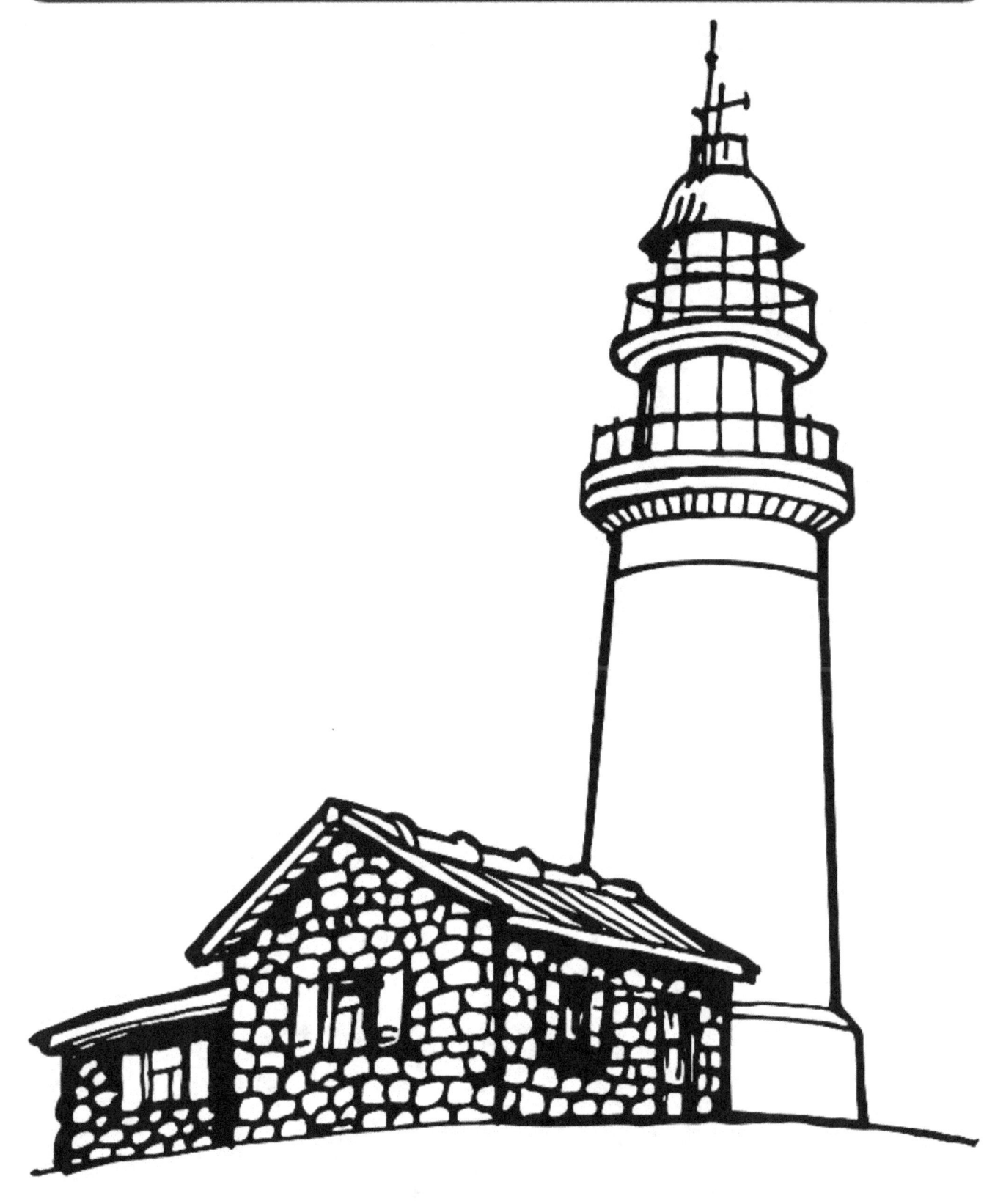

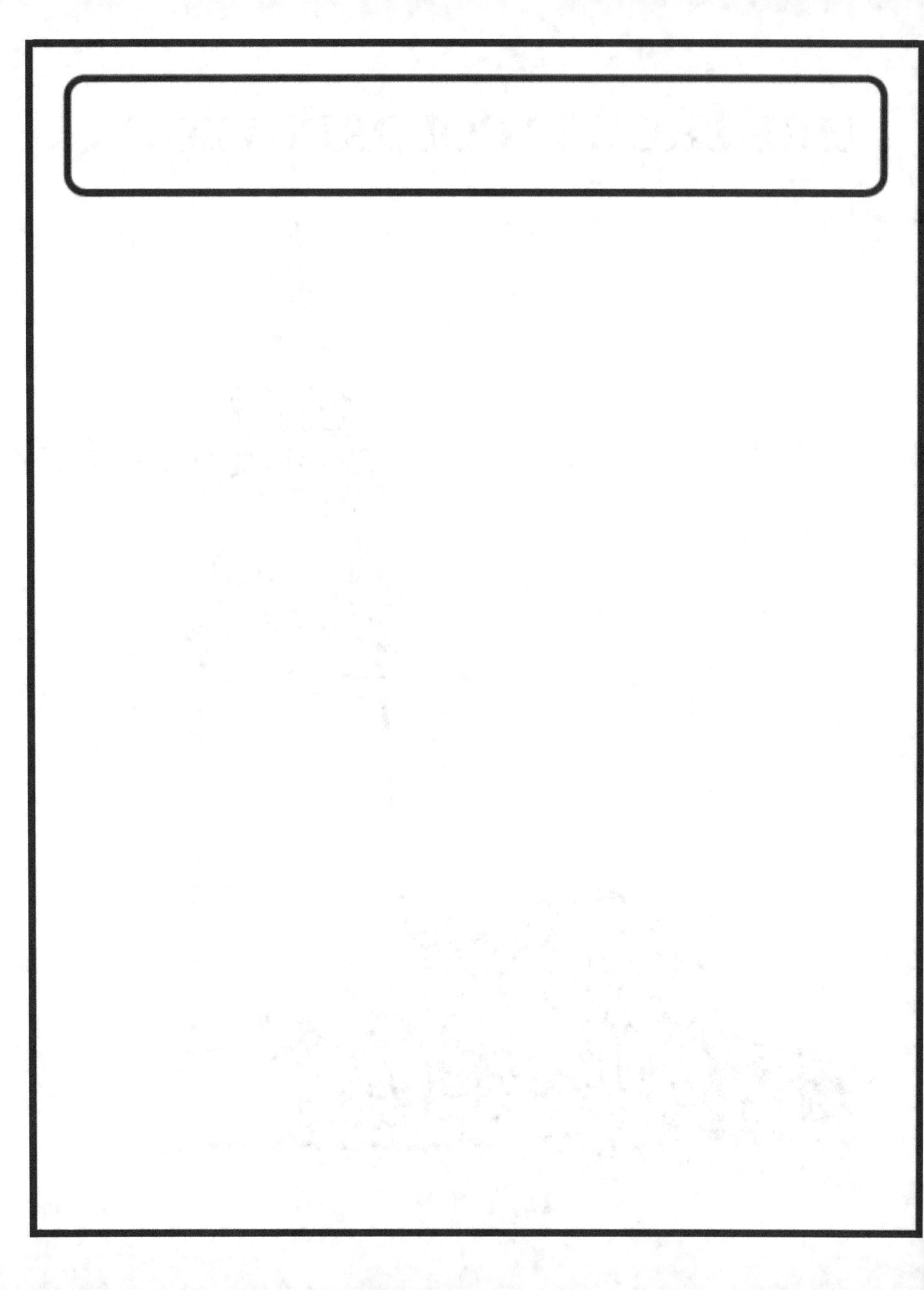

LIGHTHOUSE COLORING BOOK

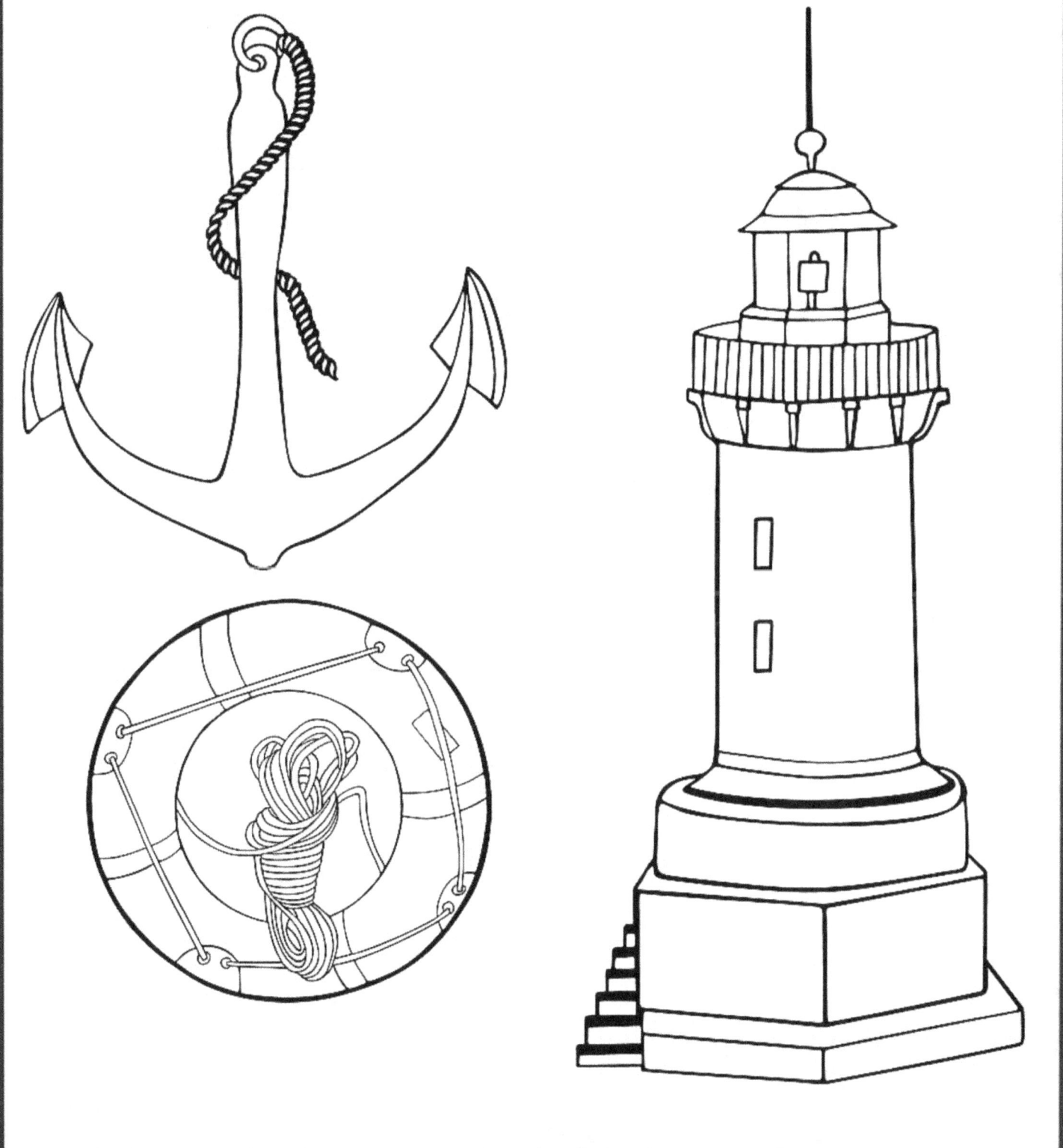

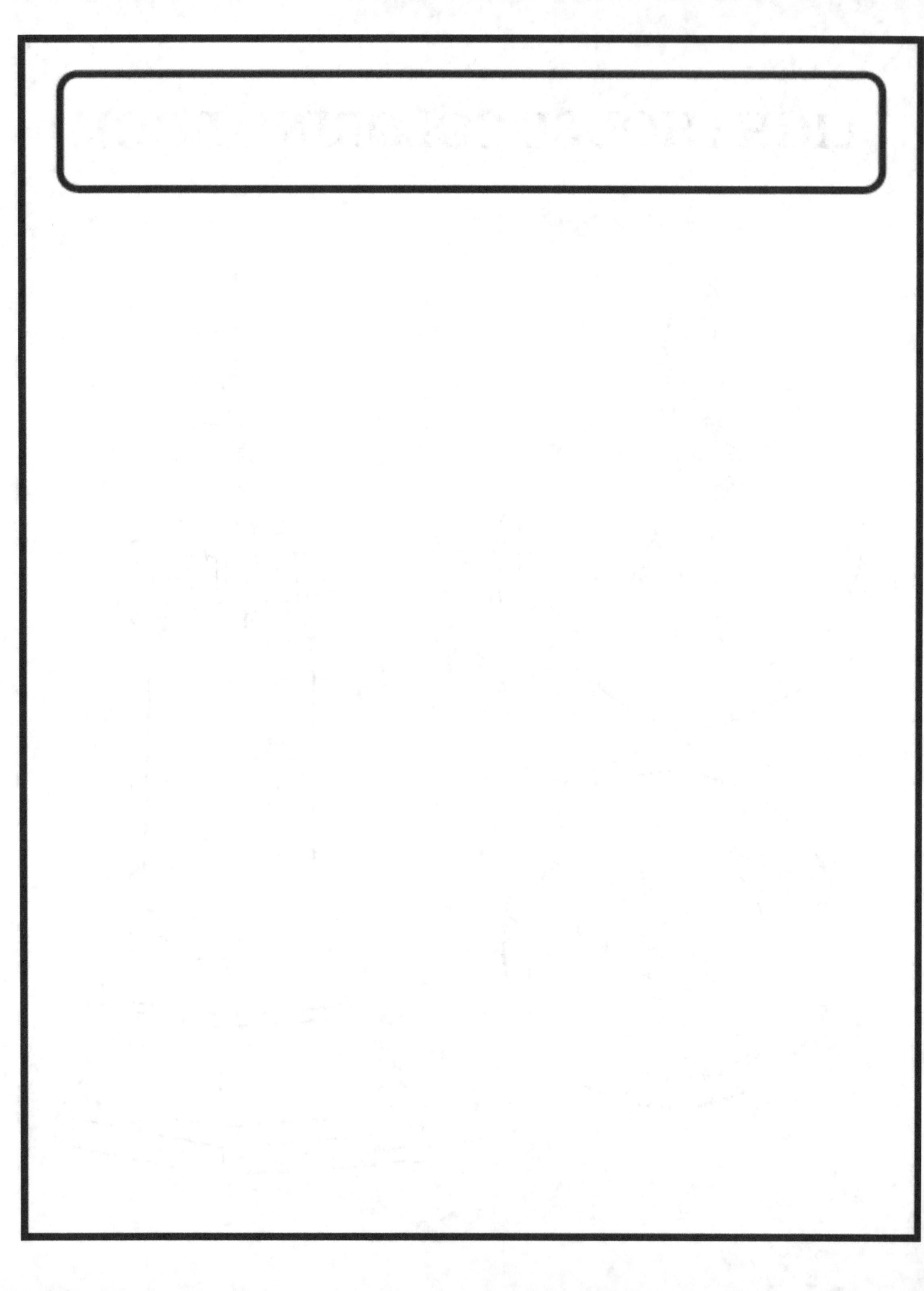

LIGHTHOUSE COLORING BOOK

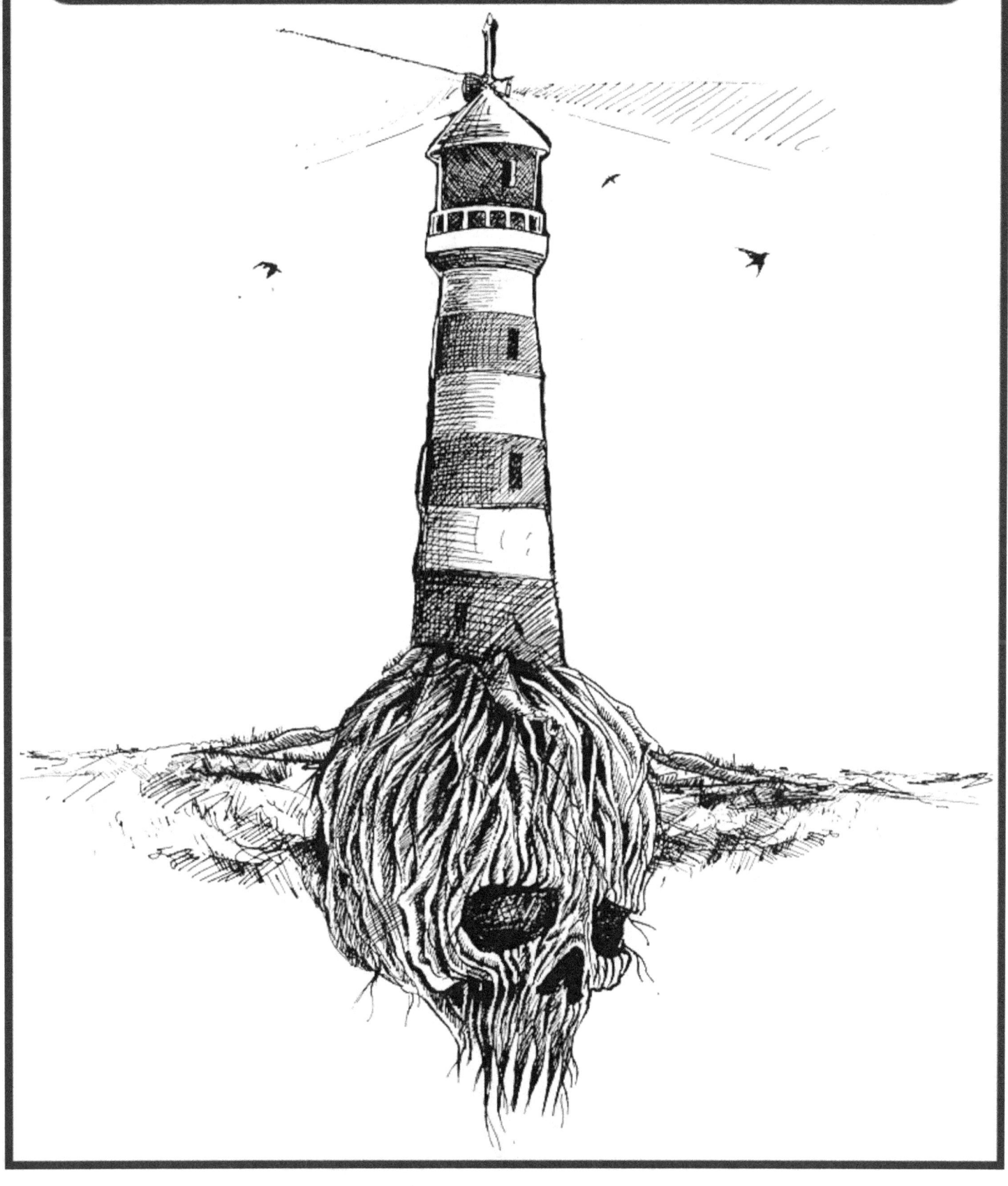

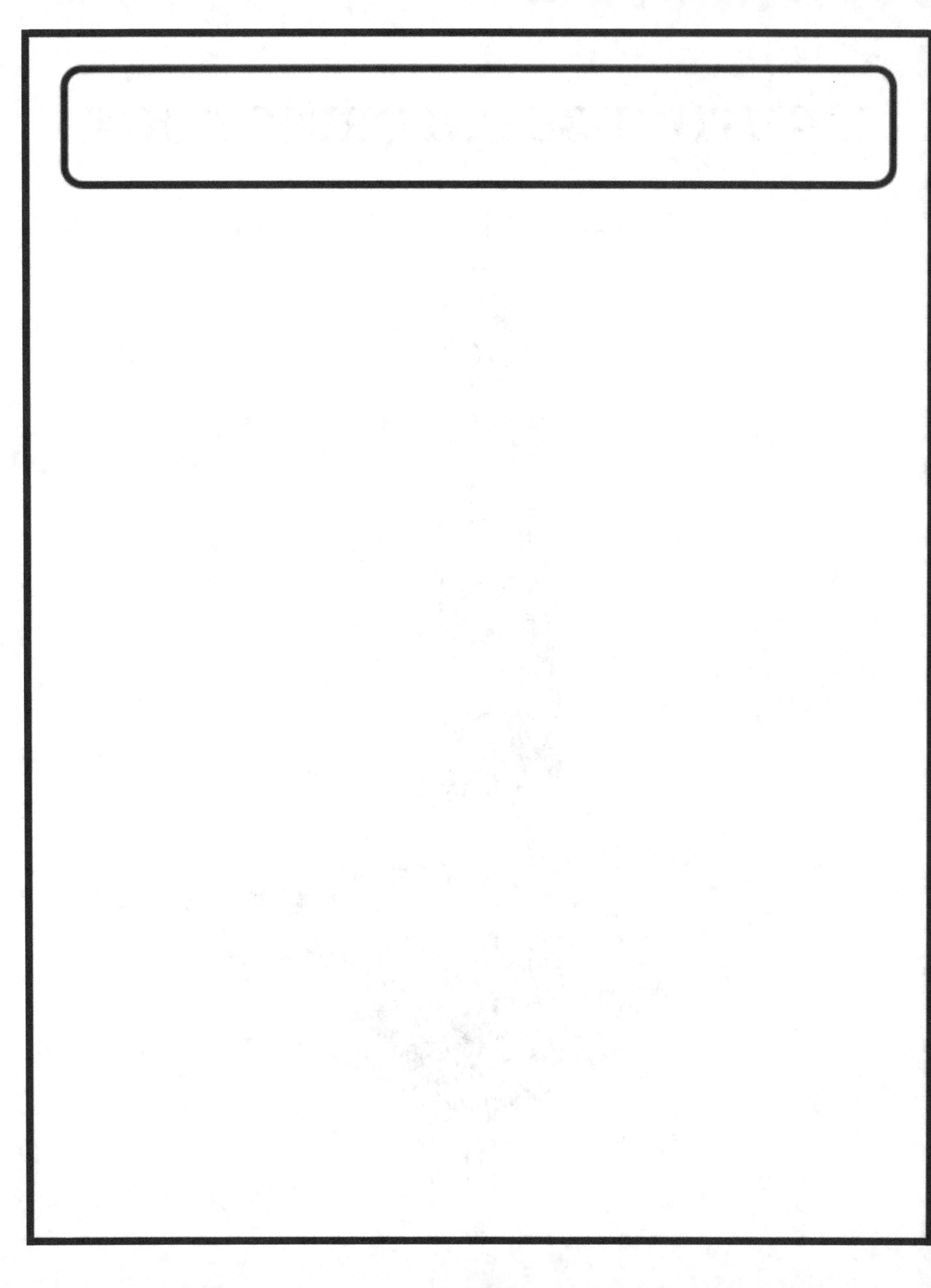

LIGHTHOUSE COLORING BOOK

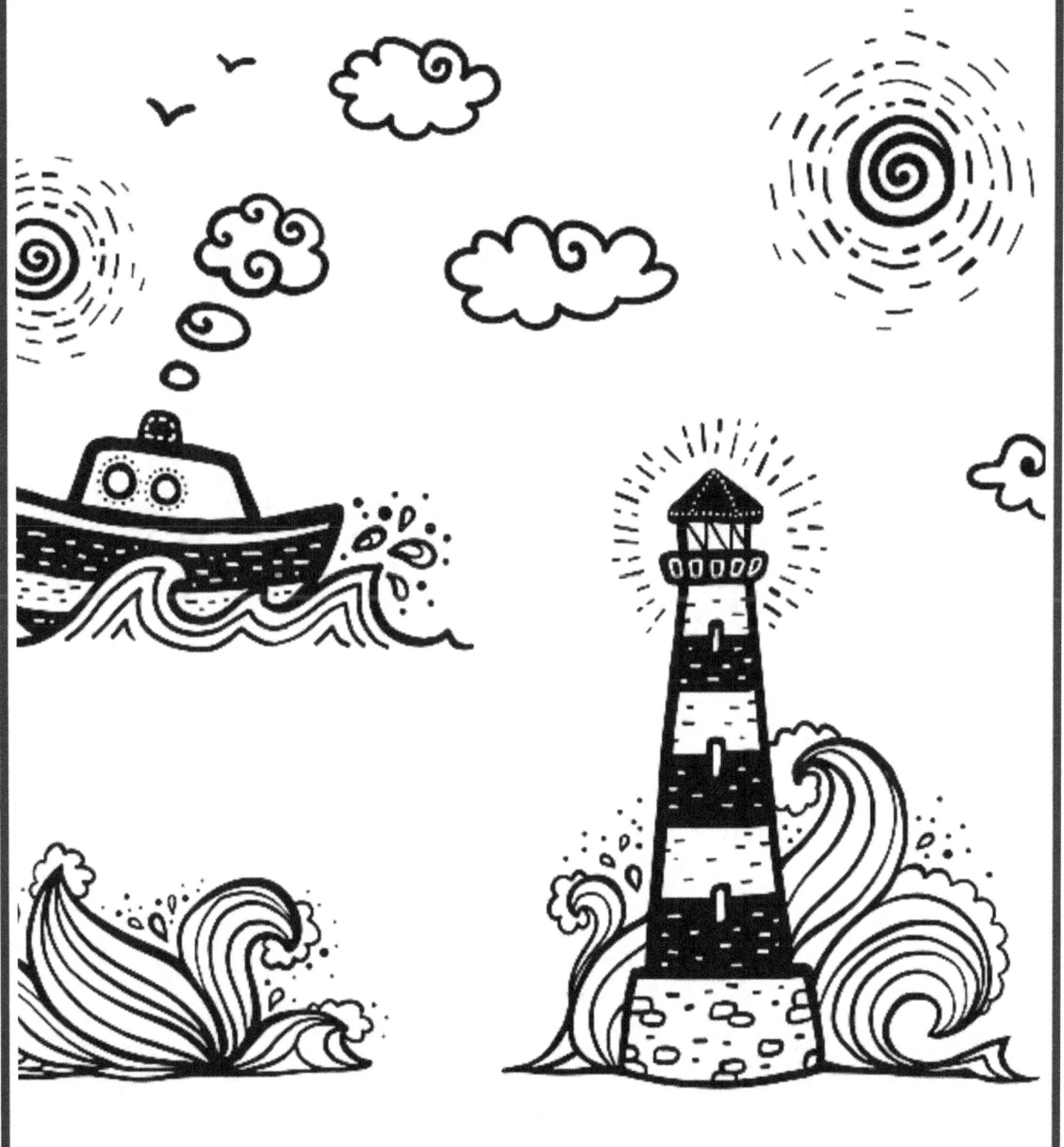

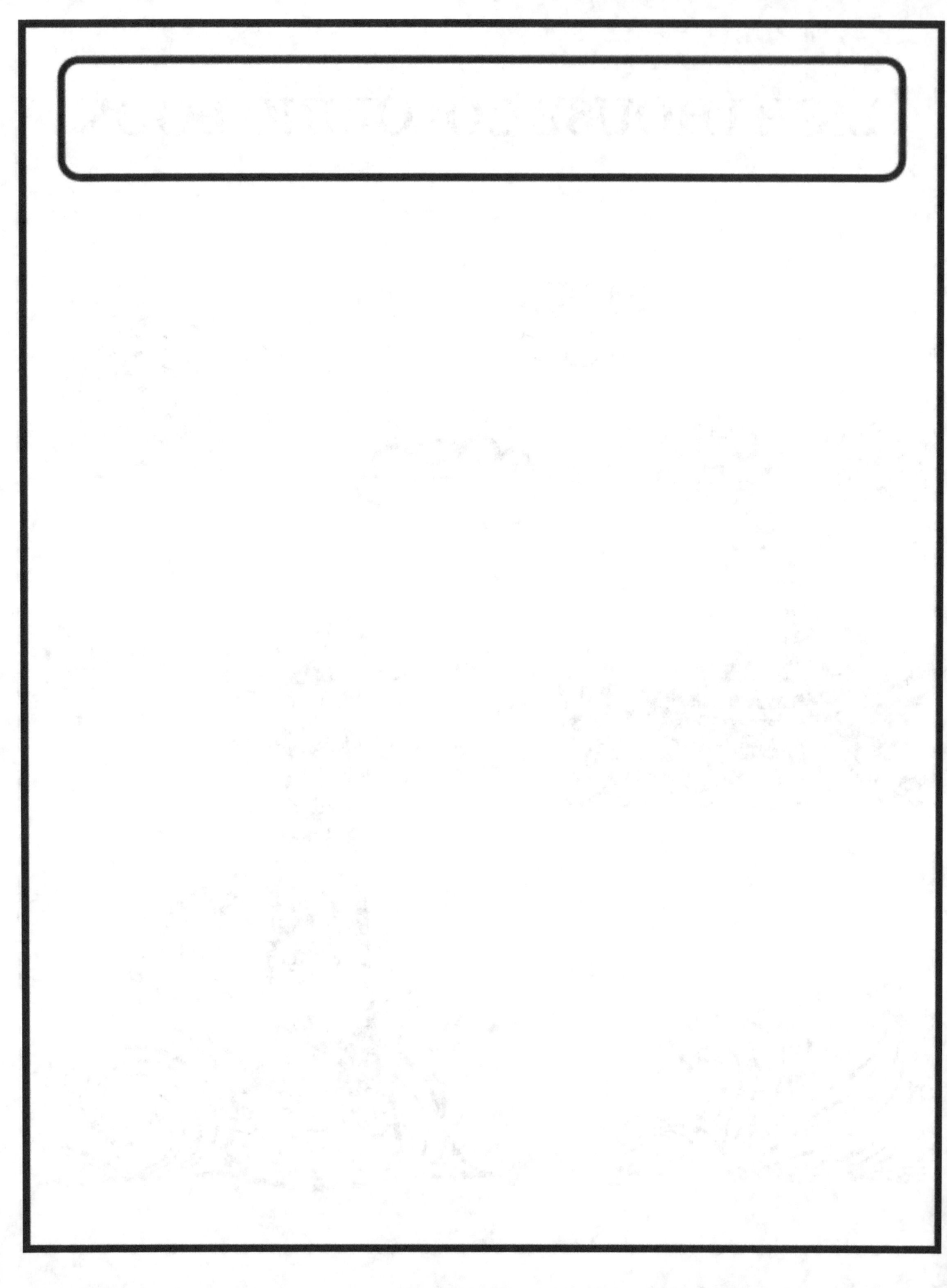

LIGHTHOUSE COLORING BOOK

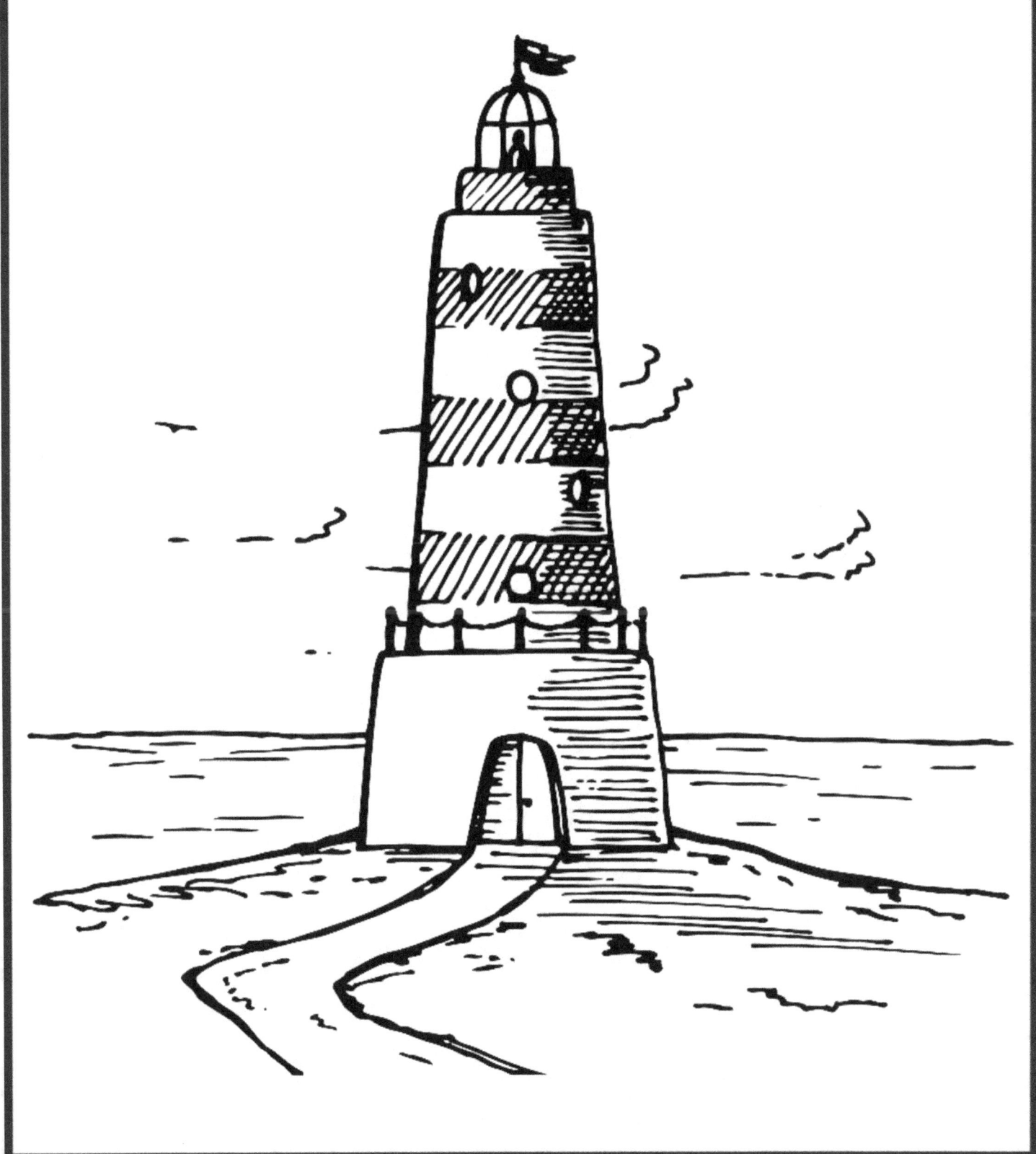

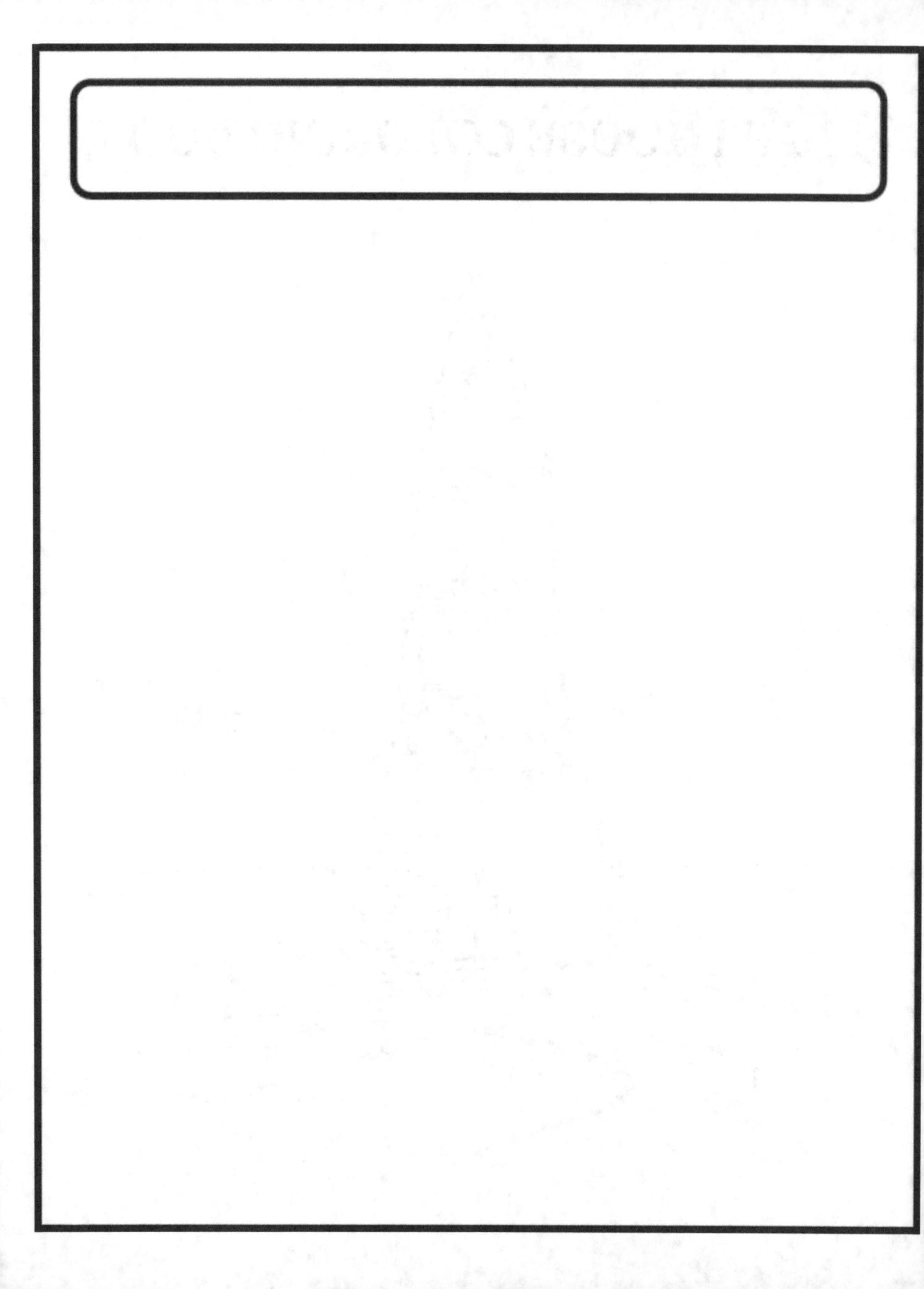

LIGHTHOUSE COLORING BOOK

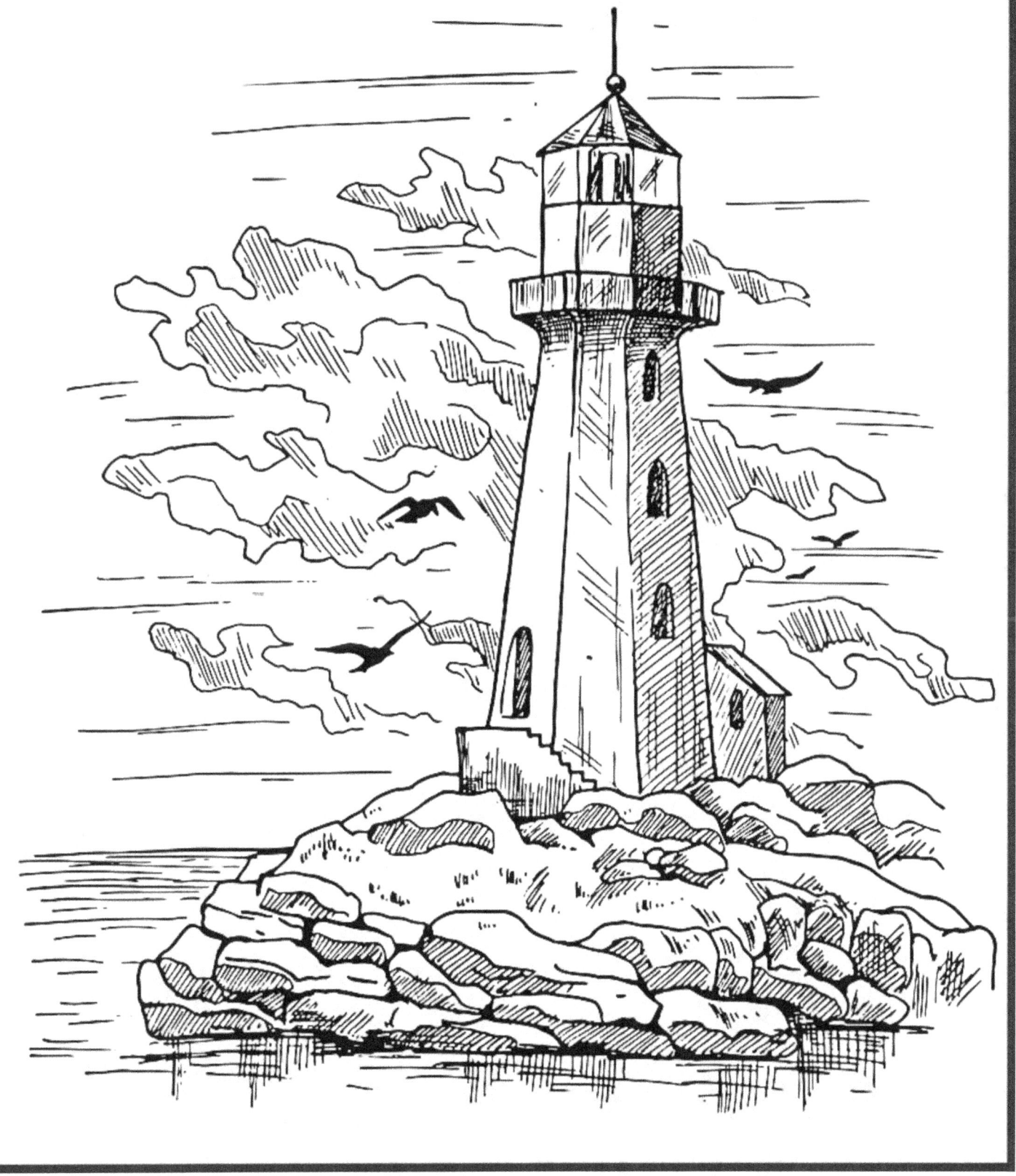

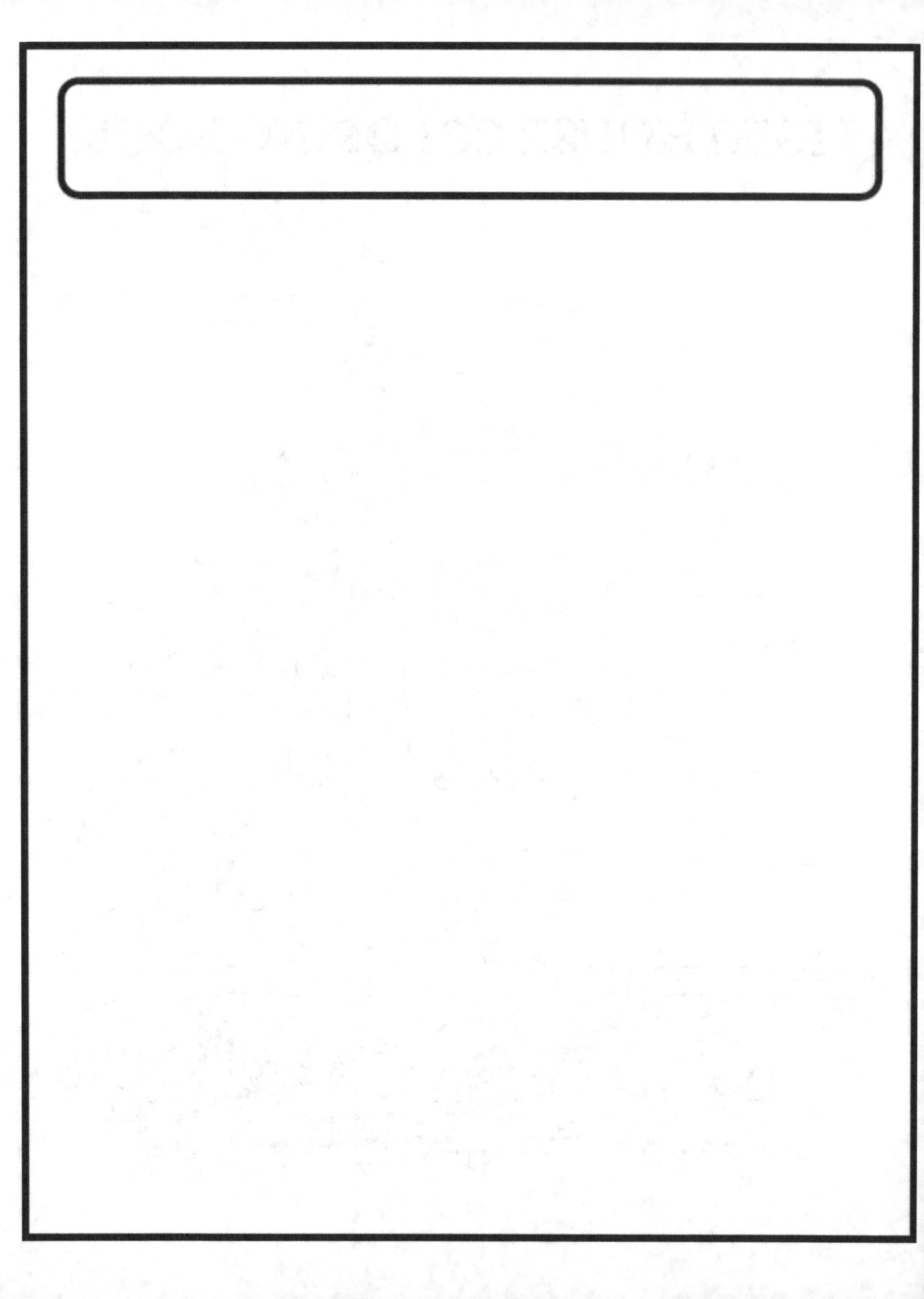

LIGHTHOUSE COLORING BOOK

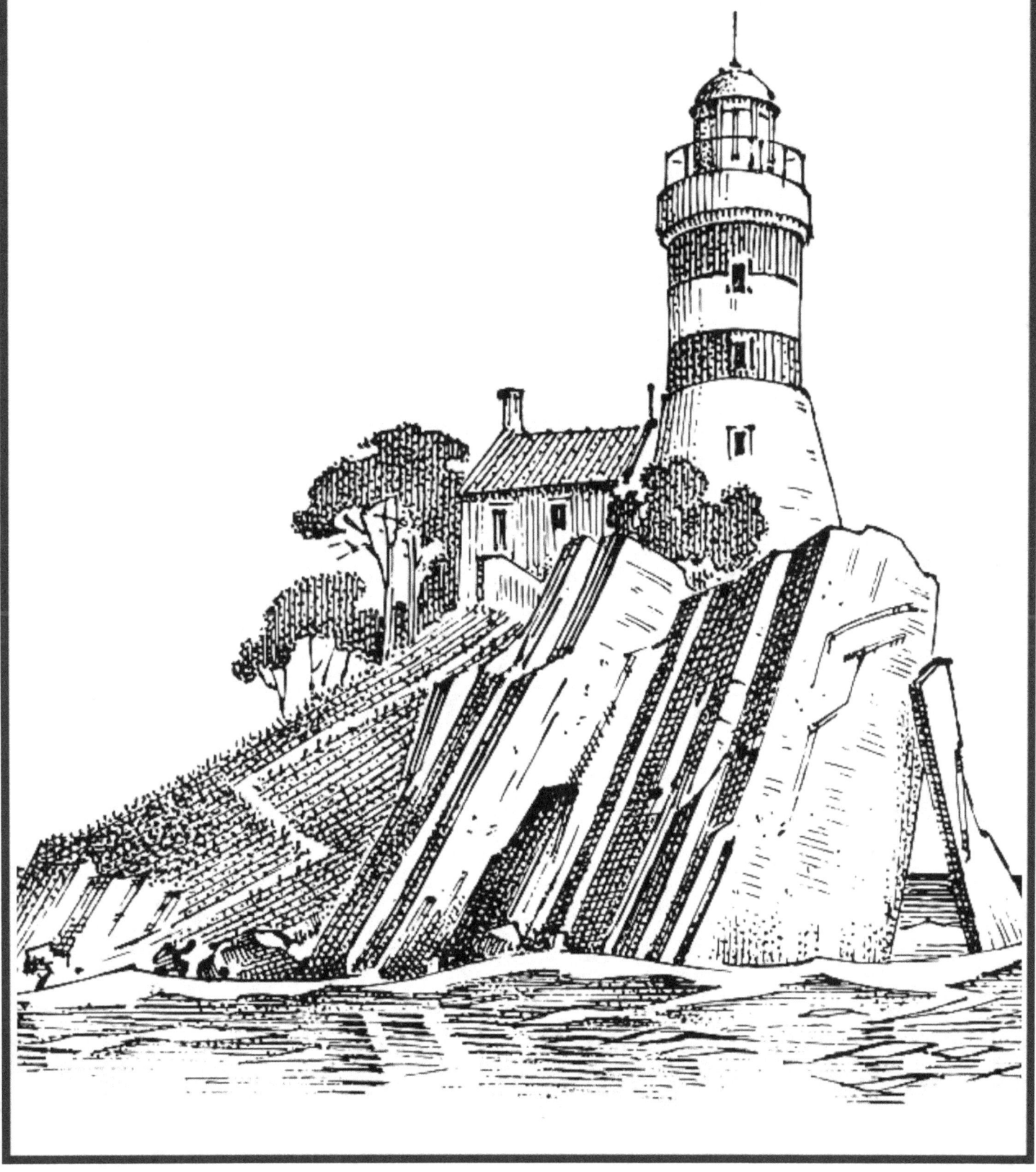

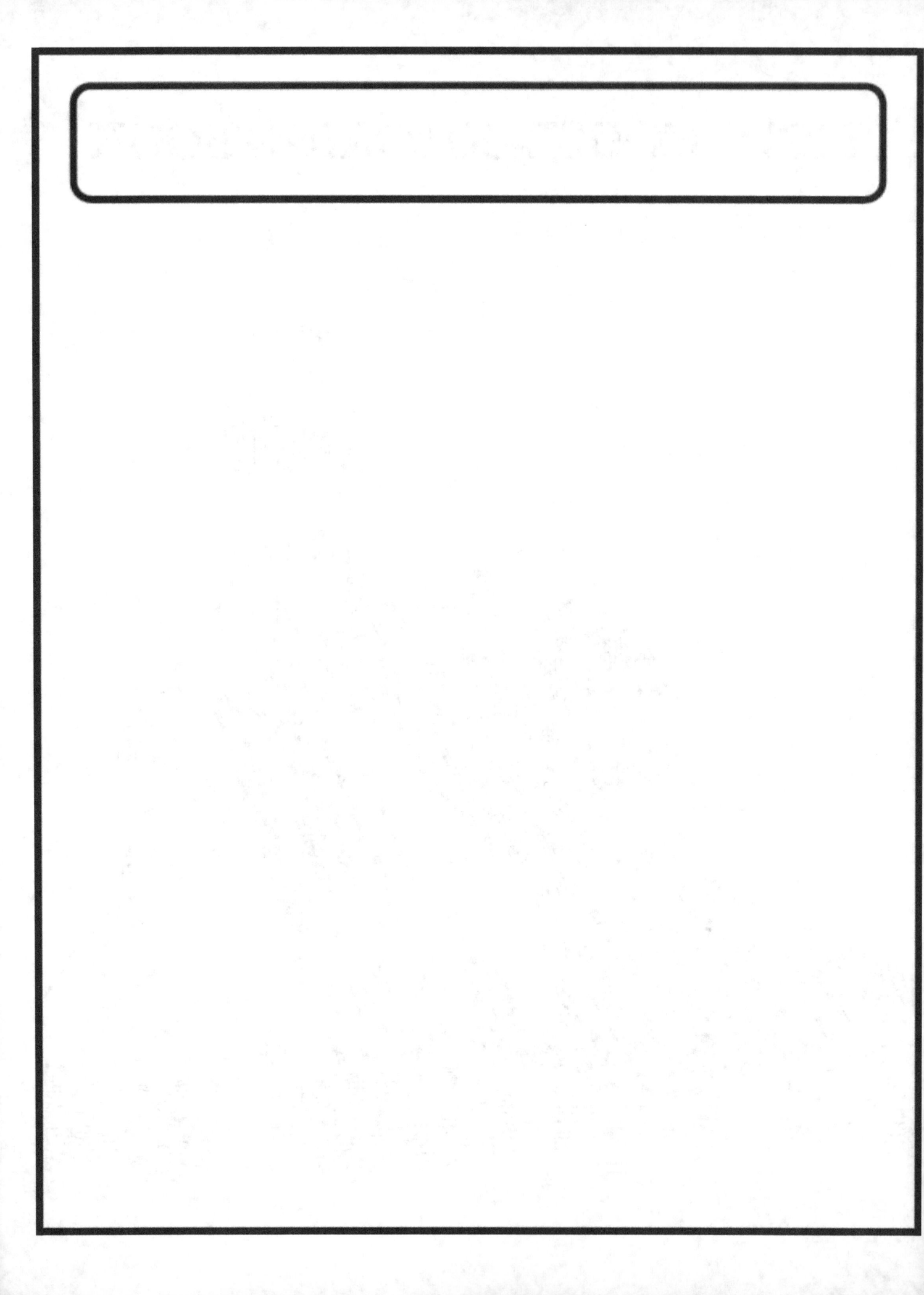

LIGHTHOUSE COLORING BOOK

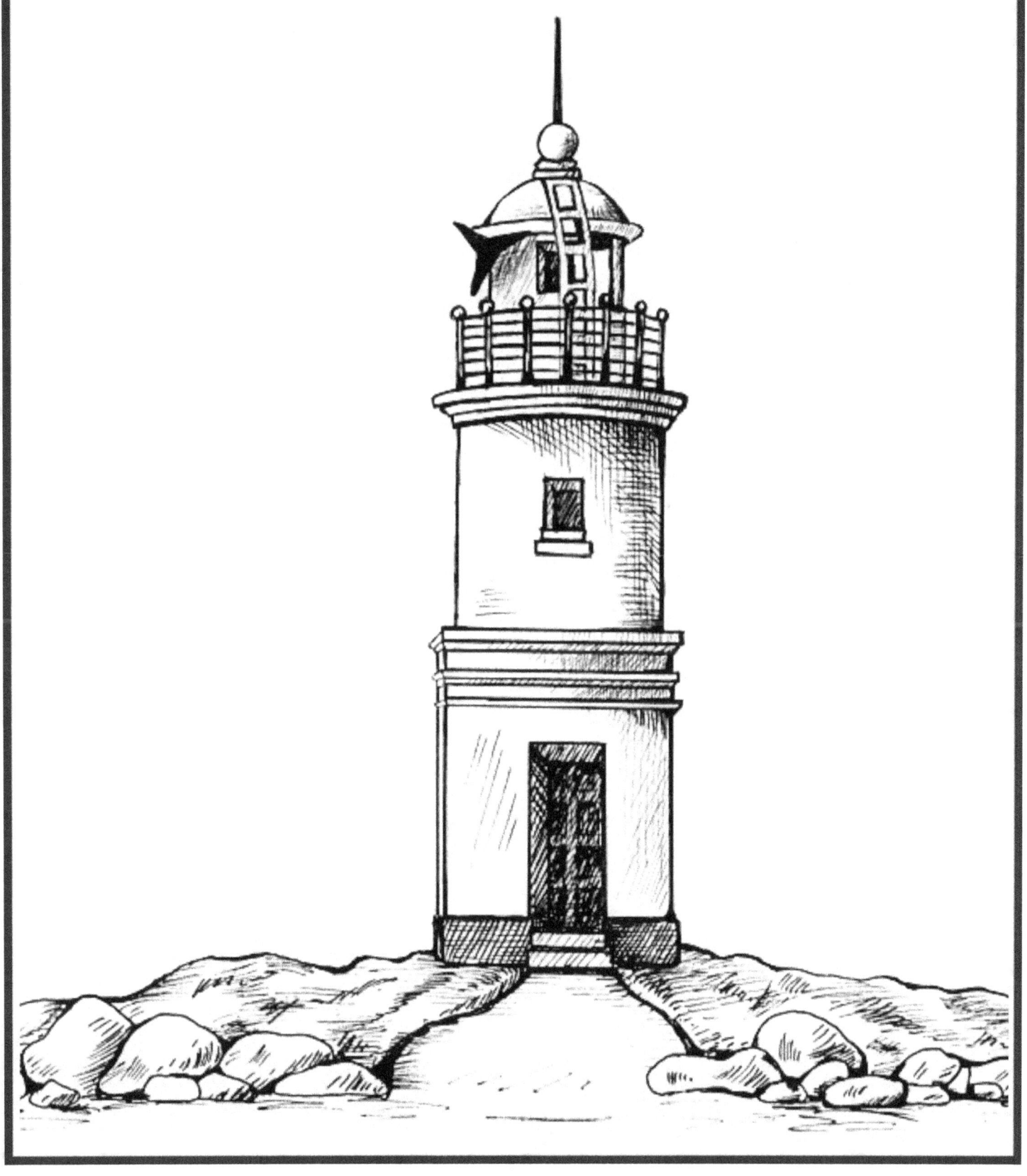

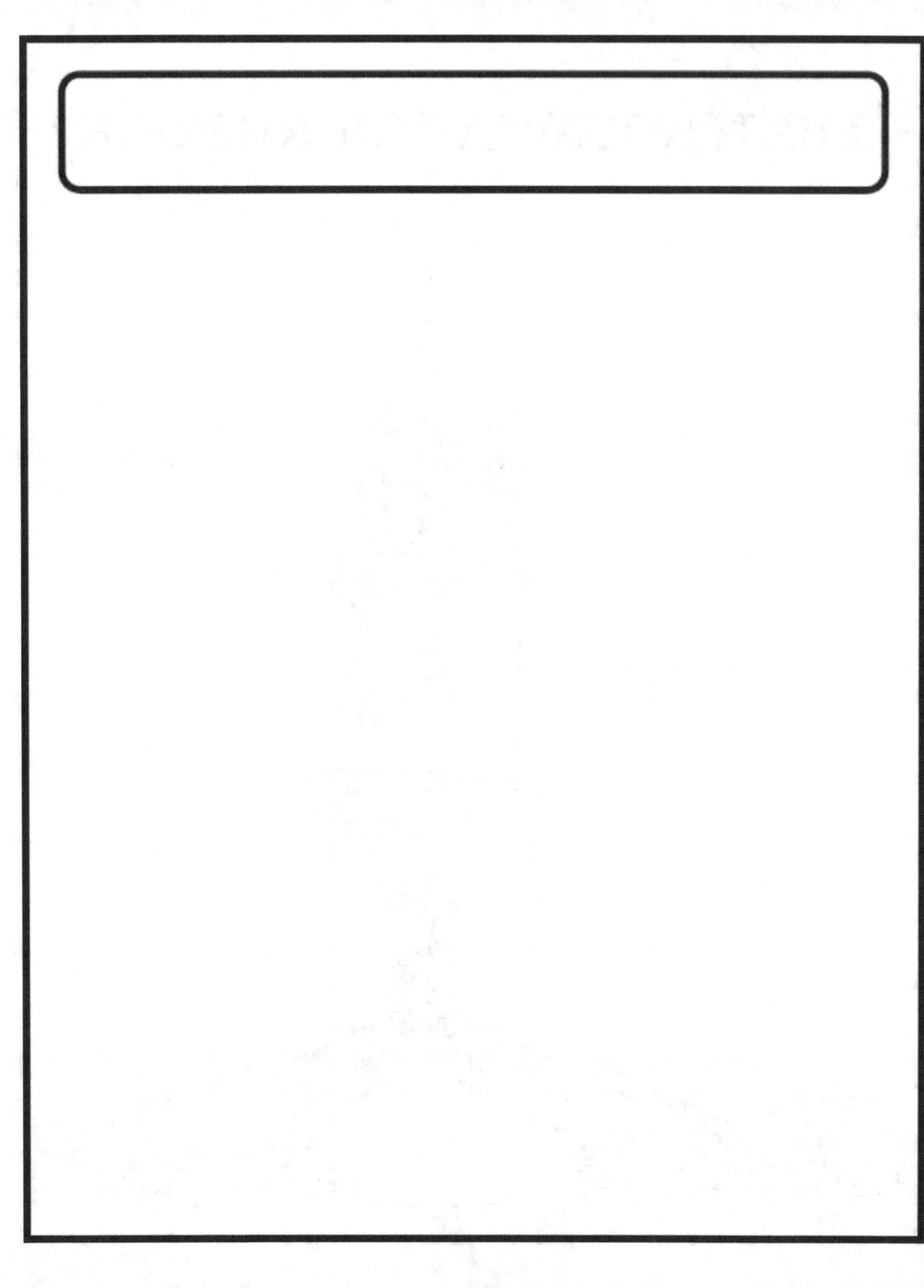

LIGHTHOUSE COLORING BOOK

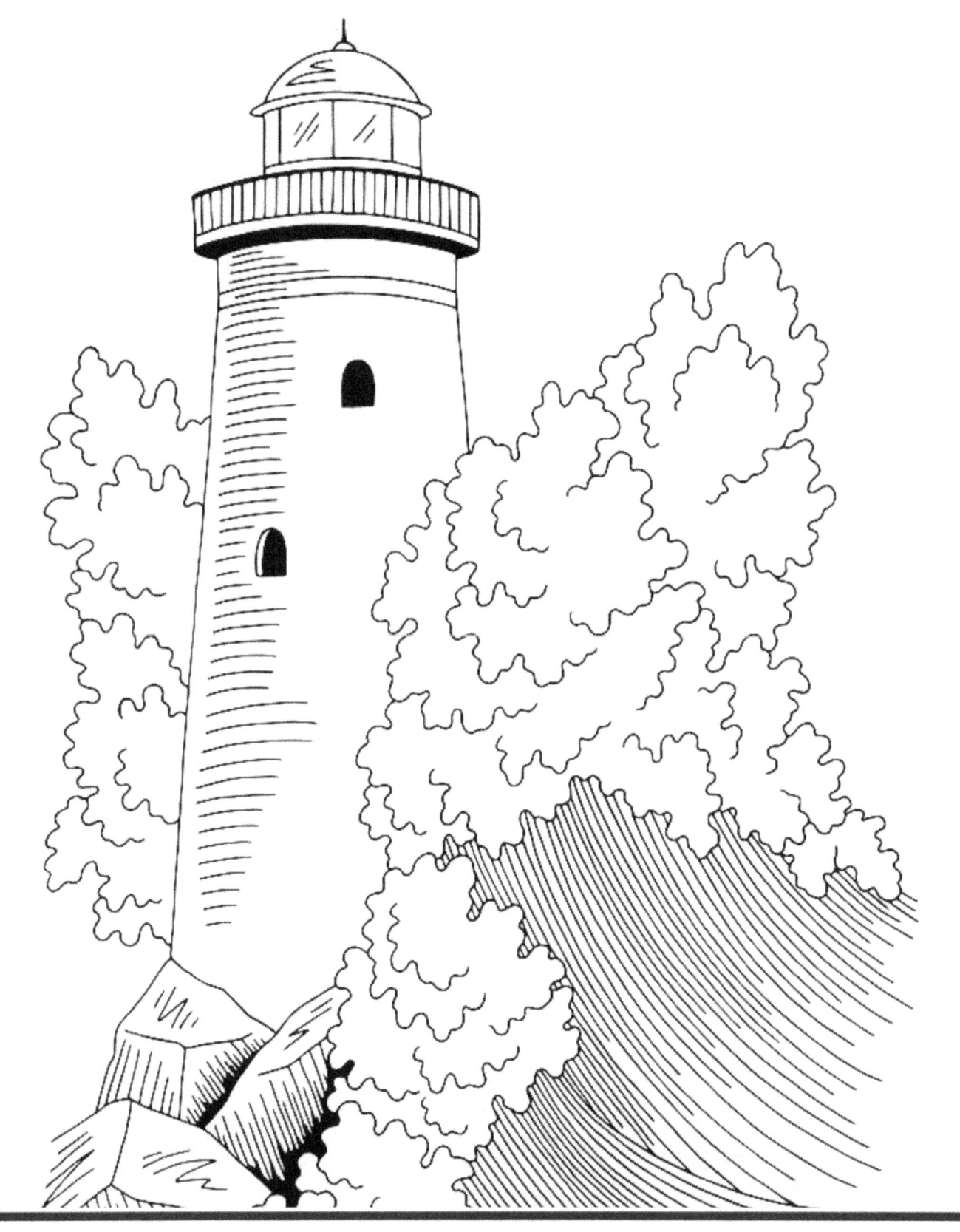

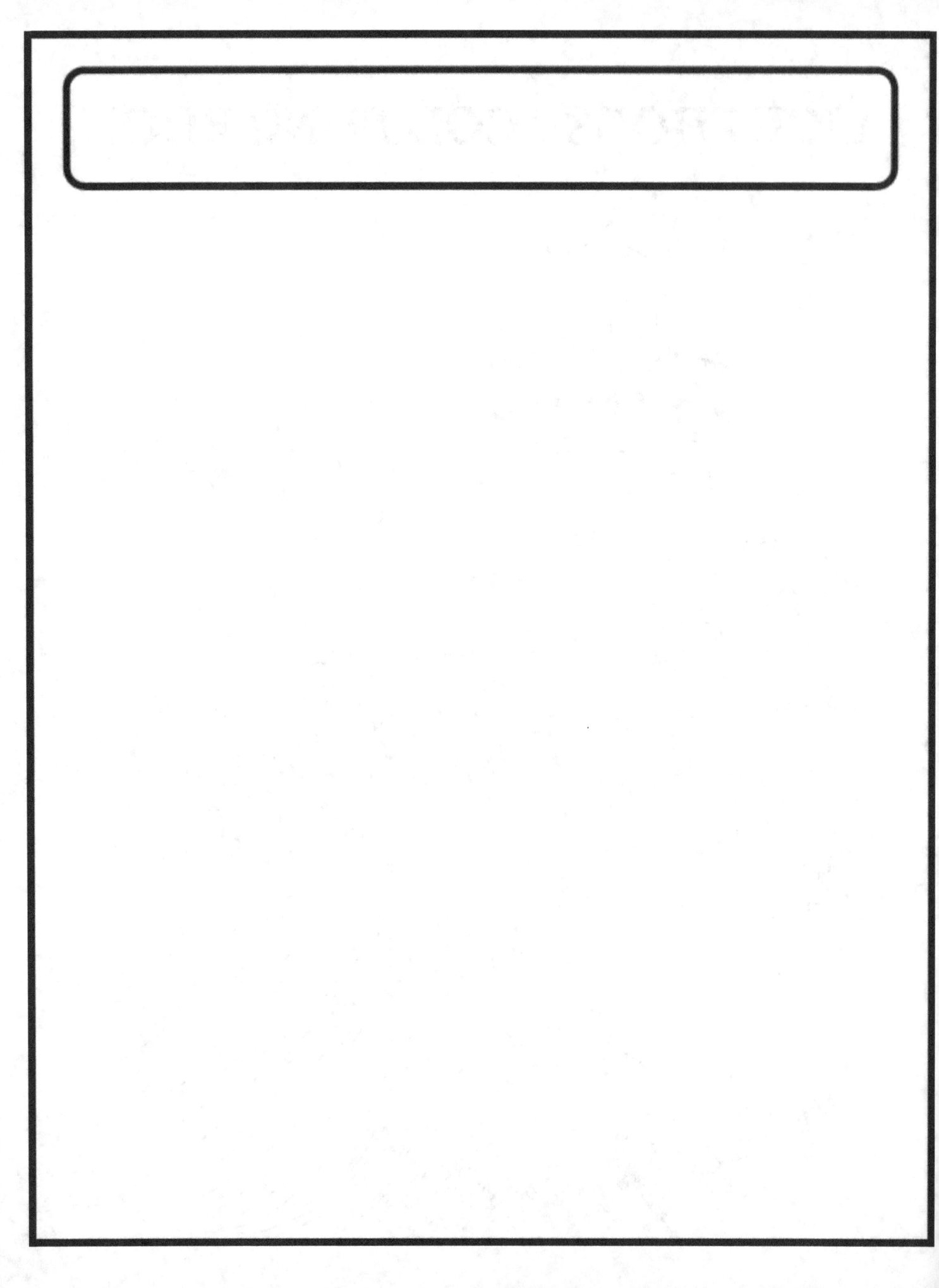

LIGHTHOUSE COLORING BOOK

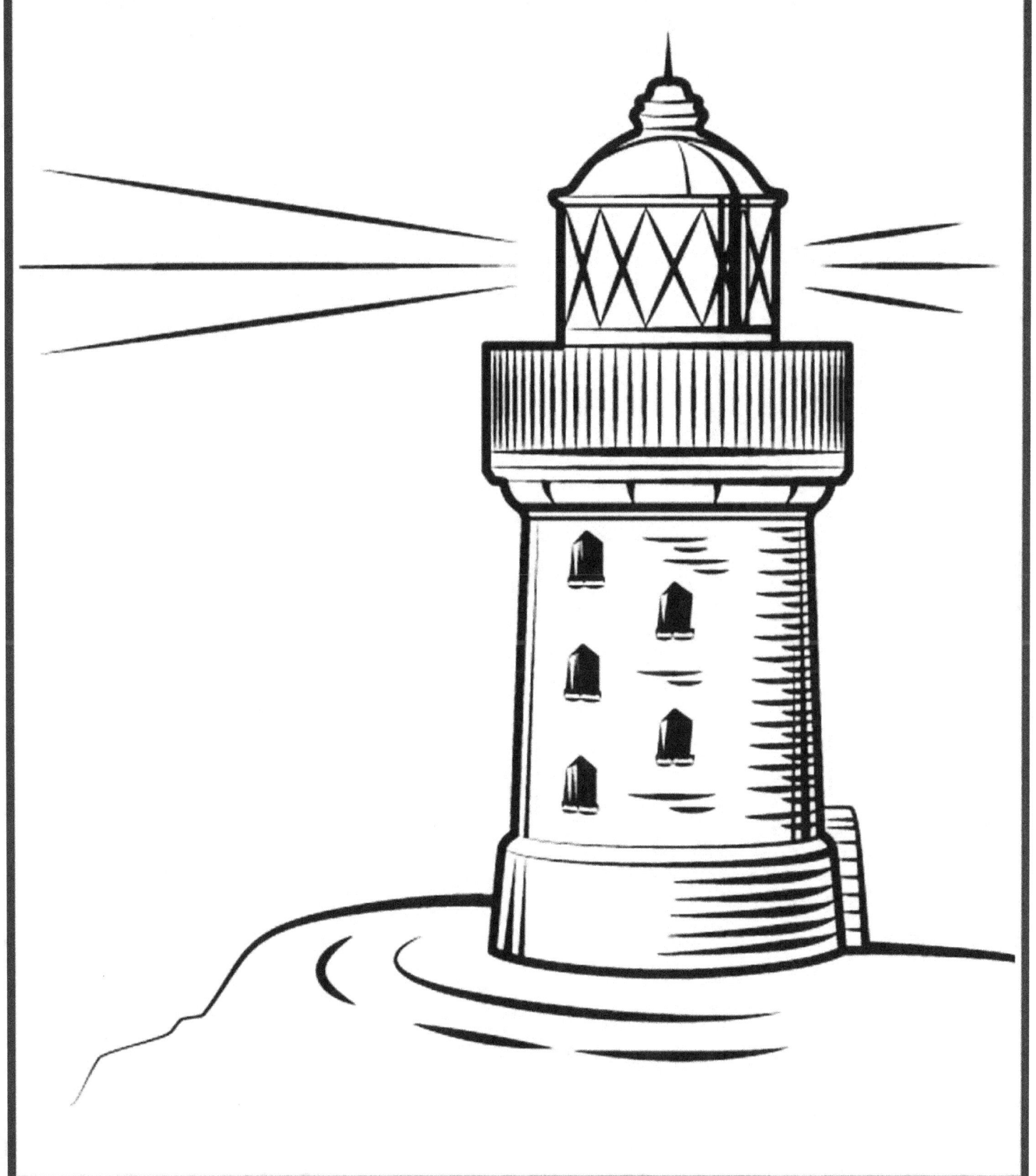

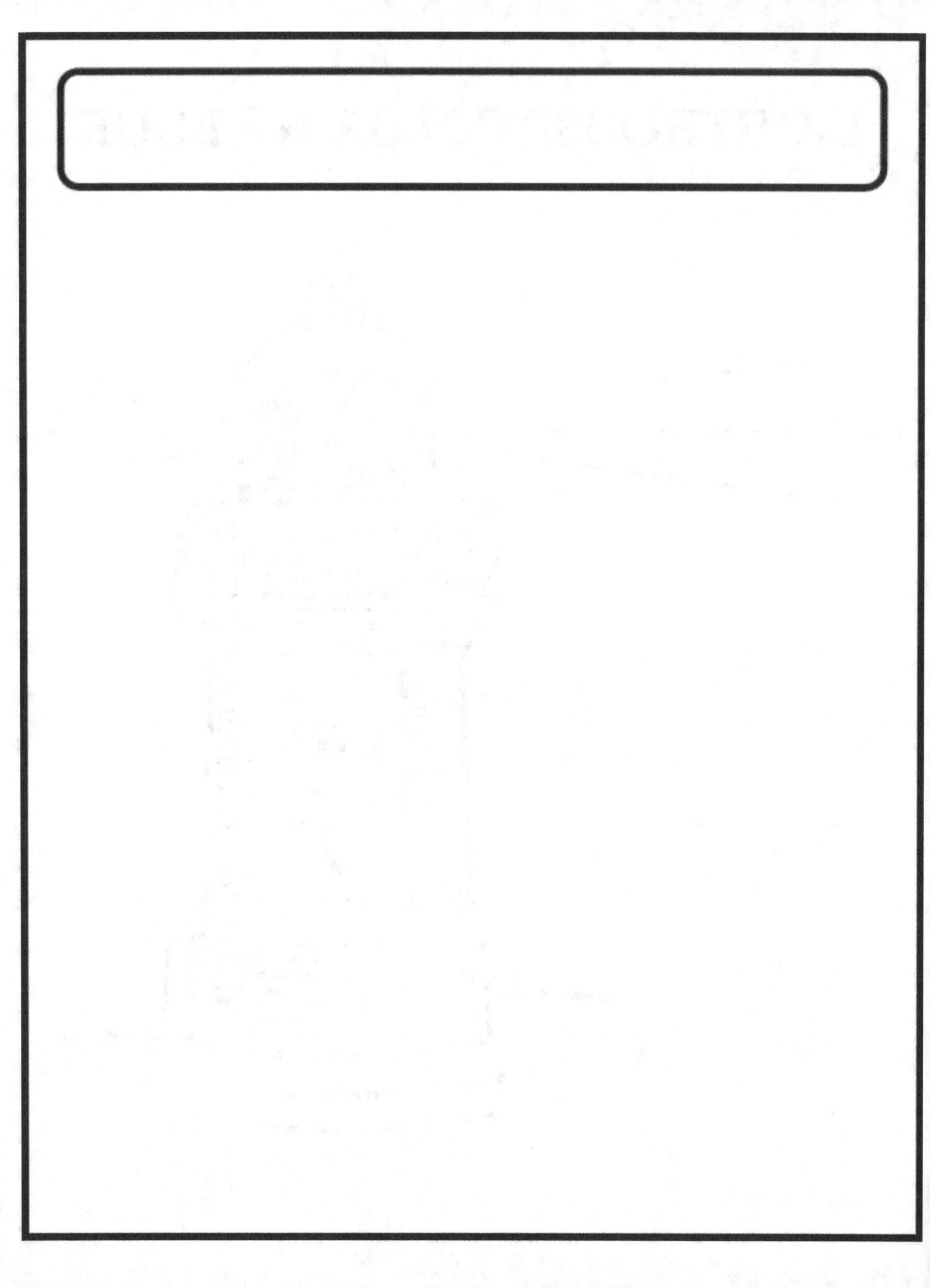

LIGHTHOUSE COLORING BOOK

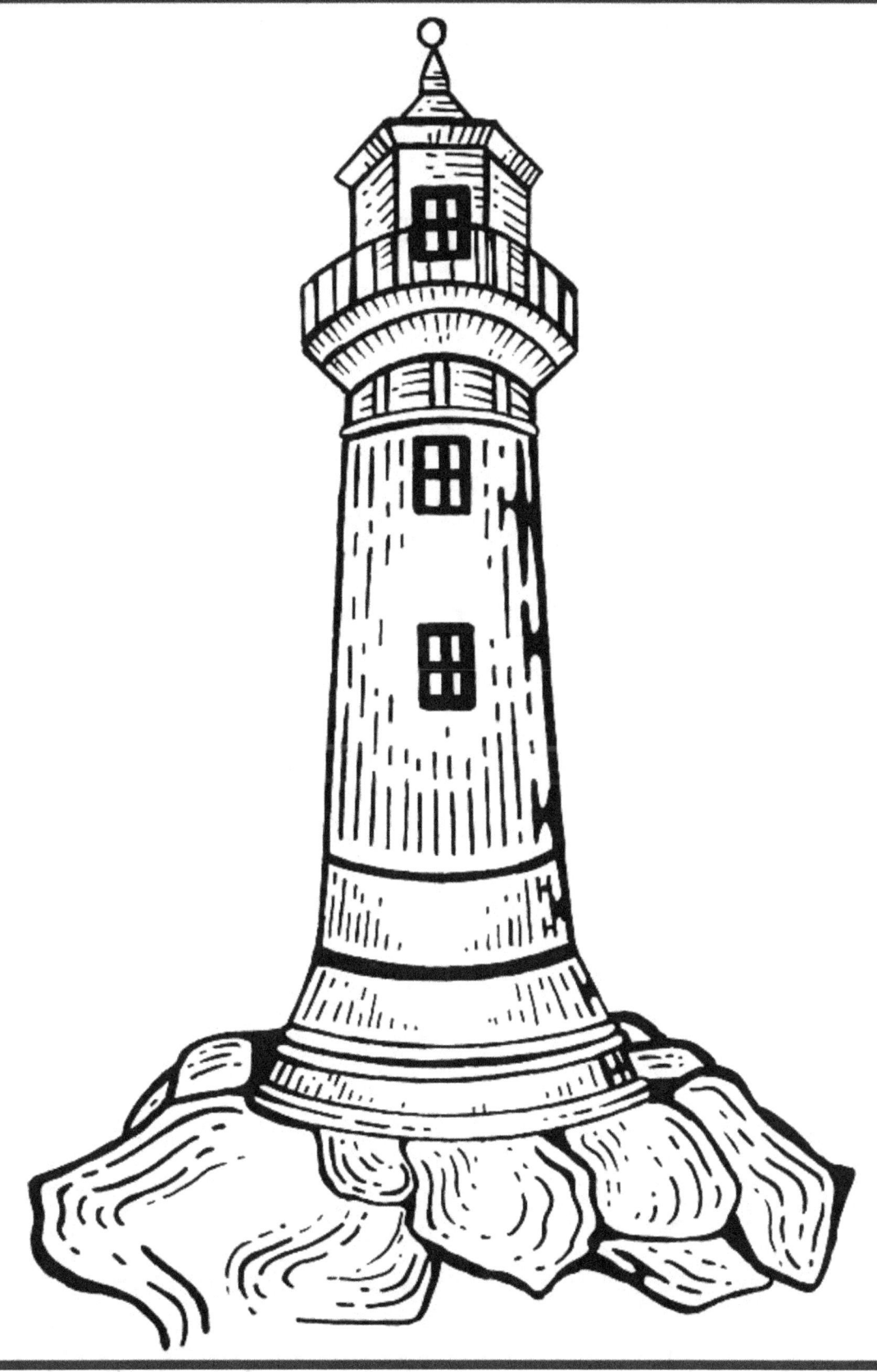

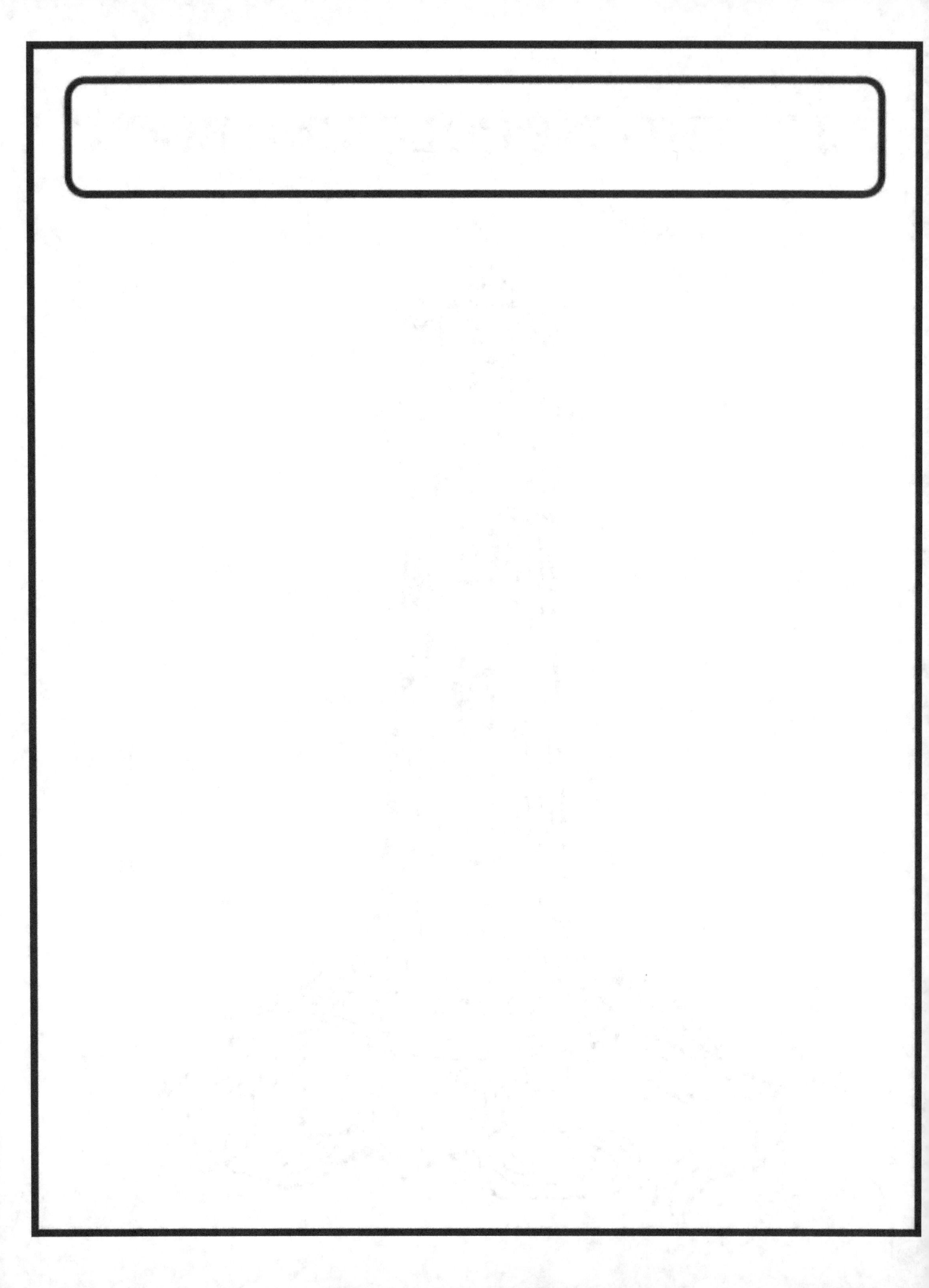

LIGHTHOUSE COLORING BOOK

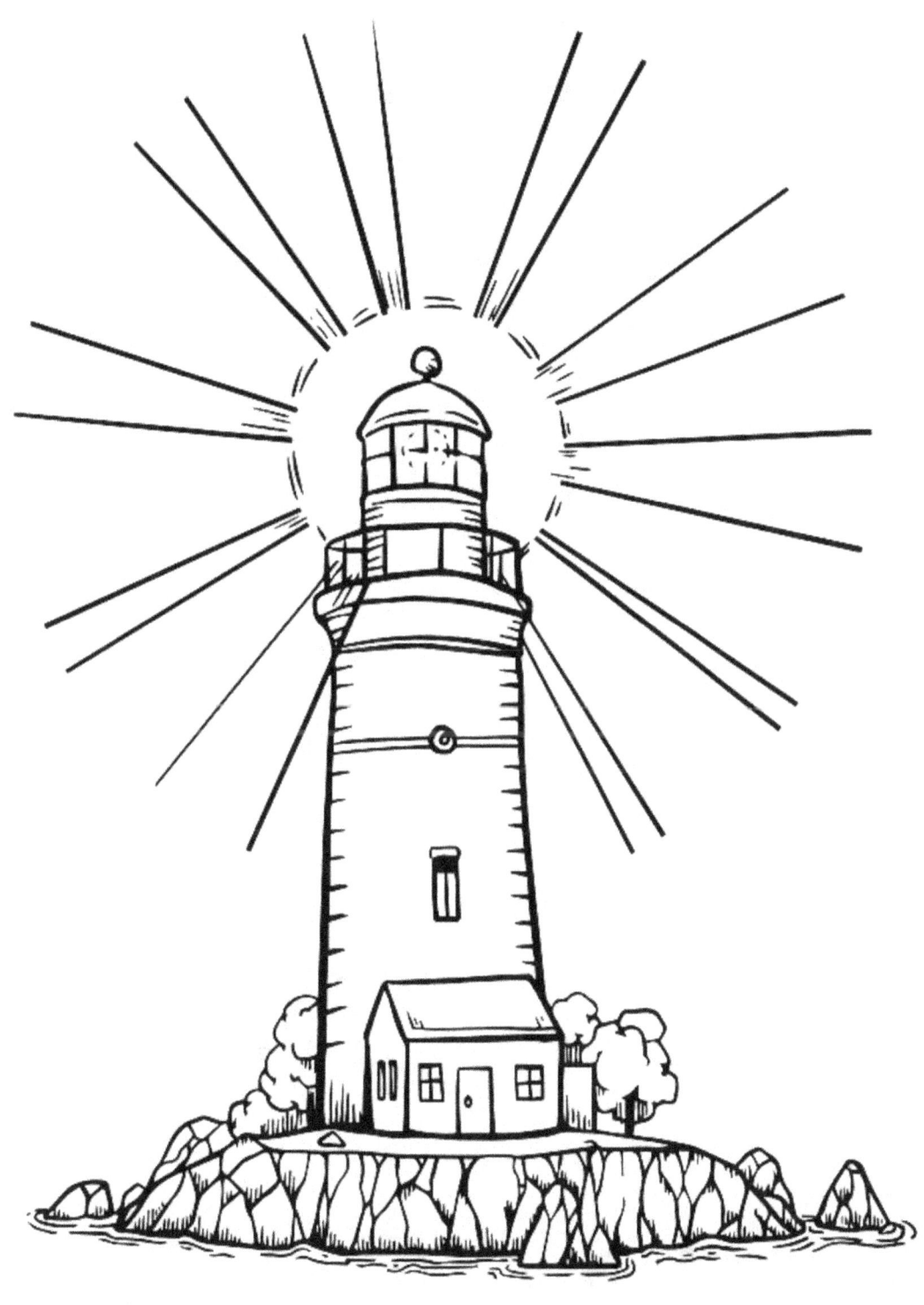

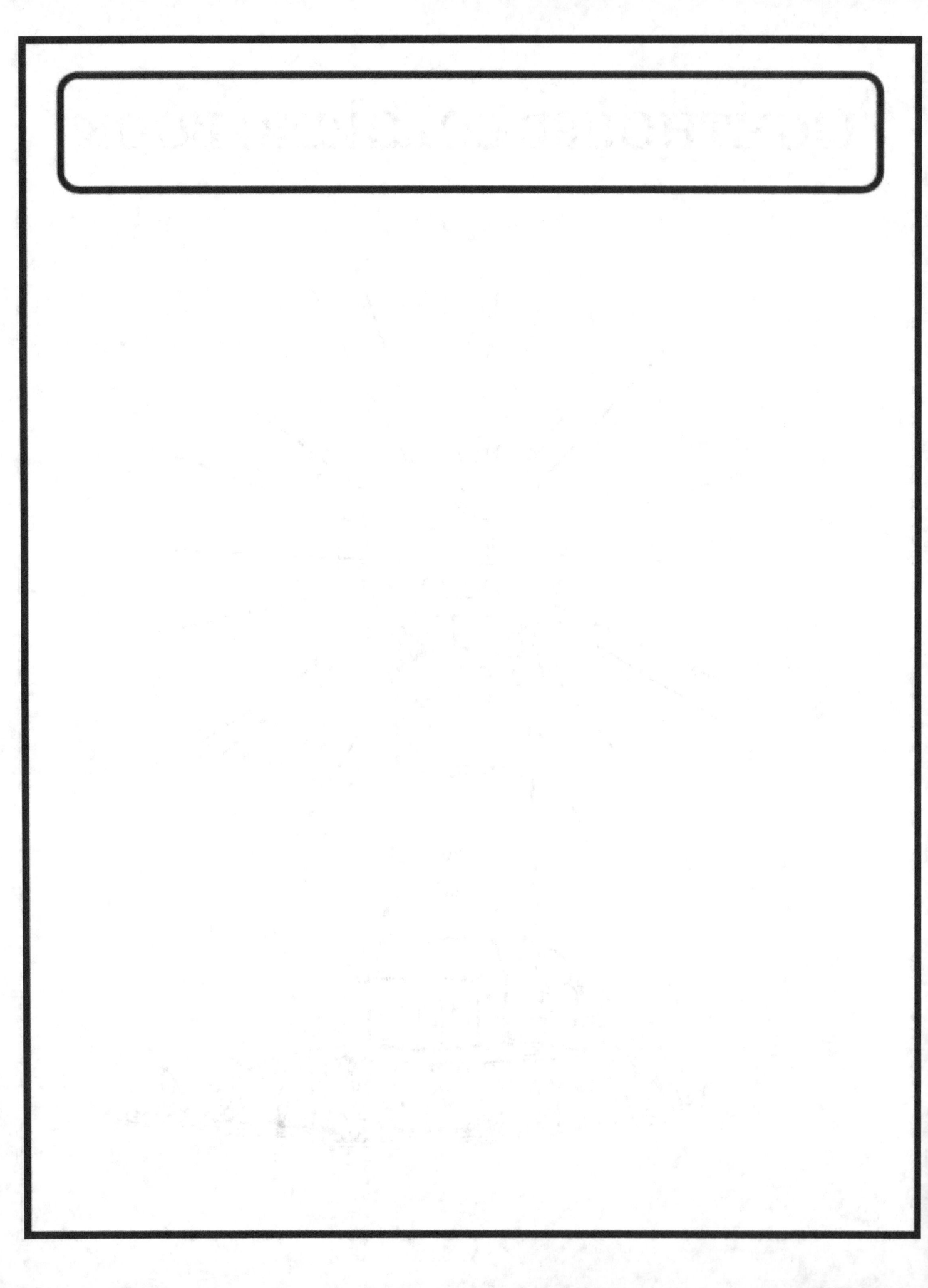

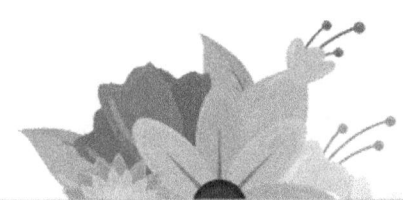

Enjoying this Notebook?

Please leave *Black Rose Press House* a review
because we would love to know your thought,
feedback, and opinions to create
better products for you.
*Please share how you creatively use your
notebooks and journals.*

THANKS
FOR YOUR SUPPORT

*Scan This Qr Code And Visit Our
Author Page At-*

amazon.com